RED SKY IN THE MORNING

The Battle of the Barents Sea,
31 December 1942

RED SKY IN THE MORNING

The Battle of the Barents Sea, 31 December 1942

MICHAEL PEARSON

Airlife

First published in the UK in 2002
by Airlife Publishing Ltd

British Library Cataloguing-in-Publication Data
  A catalogue record for this book
  is available from the British Library

ISBN 1 84037 339 3

Typeset by Phoenix Typesetting, Ilkley, West Yorkshire
Printed in England by MPG Books Ltd., Bodmin, Cornwall.

For a complete list of all Airlife titles please contact:

Airlife Publishing Ltd
101 Longden Road, Shrewsbury, SY3 9EB, England
E-mail: airlife@airlifebooks.com
Website: www.airlifebooks.com

'Watching from this locality the battle has reached its climax. I can see only red.'

Kapitänleutnant Karl-Heinz Herschelb,
U354, 11.45 hrs, 31 December 1942

For my parents Marie and Leslie,
who lived through those years

ACKNOWLEDGEMENTS

I would like to extend my sincere thanks to the following persons and organisations without whom this book would not have been possible. I would particularly like to thank the veterans, British and German, who contributed their recollections and expertise with such unfailing enthusiasm and good humour.

Mr Smith Belford
Bundesarchiv, Koblenz (Researcher Dr Ekkehart Guth)
Lieutenant-Commander J.P. Donovan
Radio Mate and Guard Commander Johann Hengel
Captain Michael Hutton
Imperial War Museum, London
Mrs Pamela Marchant, for permission to use the taped
    interview with Lieutenant-Commander T.J. Marchant
Commander Loftus Peyton-Jones
Public Records Office, London
Mrs Helen Rhead, for permission to use the memoir of
    Lieutenant-Commander Eric Rhead
Control Telephone Officer for Heavy Artillery Josef Schmitz
Lieutenant-Commander A.W. Twiddy
Leading Stoker Walter Watkin

I would also like to express my appreciation to Mike Taylor, my good friend and fellow history buff, for his invaluable help in checking the drafts and proofs.

Mike Pearson

CONTENTS

MAPS AND DIAGRAMS

ILLUSTRATIONS

INTRODUCTION

On 31 December 1942, the icy expanse of the Barents Sea witnessed a naval battle which all but ended offensive operations by the heavy ships of the German navy for the remainder of the war. How this came to be is firmly rooted in the psyche of Adolf Hitler. Military hardware of all kinds held a fascination for Germany's *Führer*, and it was inevitable that he would be drawn to the tremendous power of the heavy ships of his navy, both as weapons of war, and for the prestige and influence which they attracted to the *Reich* from abroad.

His attitude to the navy in general, however, was complex, and can be traced back to Germany's defeat in 1918. A significant factor in that defeat, Hitler believed, had been the mutiny of the High Seas Fleet, and as such he never totally trusted the navy. It is probably also fair to say that he was not navy-minded, having little understanding of the complexities of naval warfare; and was, compared with land operations, unsure of himself when dealing with the war at sea. In a moment of unusual self-criticism, he remarked that he considered himself a lion on land but a coward at sea.

The naval war began badly for the German surface fleet, with the loss of the pocket battleship *Admiral Graf Spee* in December 1939, and, although there can be no doubt that the officers and men of the heavy ships fought with as much skill and determination as any other branch of the German armed forces, Hitler's apprehension over the fate of his major warships grew, fuelled in May 1941 by the destruction of the 'unsinkable' *Bismarck*.

In December 1942, the defeat in the Barents Sea of Vice-Admiral Kummetz's powerful battle group, at the hands of a small force of destroyers and two light cruisers, was the last straw. That this defeat was due, in part, to restrictions placed on the commander at sea by a naval high command well aware of his unease over the possibility of loss or damage to the heavy ships was ignored, and Hitler's mood turned to fury. For him, all ships of the German navy above the size of destroyers were now a useless waste of men and *matériel*, and were to be scrapped. Ultimately this large scale scrapping did not take place, however most of the ships in question were decommissioned, and following the Battle of the Barents Sea, only one offensive operation was undertaken by a German heavy ship – the abortive sortie by *Scharnhorst*, also in the Barents Sea, one year later.

CHAPTER 1

RUSSIAN ROULETTE

On 30 January 1933 Adolf Hitler became Chancellor of Germany, and within days called a meeting of senior Nazi officials and officers of the armed forces. He declared to his bemused but enthused audience that 'the conquest of the land in the east [principally Soviet Russia] and its ruthless Germanization',[1] was his unshakable and unalterable goal. If ever a man carried with him the seeds of his own destruction it was Germany's new *Führer*.

In succeeding years, Hitler's expansionism in Europe brought him into conflict with the interests of Britain and France, and realising that he could not fight a war on his eastern and western fronts at the same time, by 1939 he had concluded a non-aggression pact with Soviet Premier Stalin, intended to keep Russia quiet while he finalised military operations in the west. The *Führer* remarked that the pact was 'an entente, in short, watched over by an eagle eye and with a finger on the trigger',[2] amply illustrating his attitude both to the pact and to Russia. For his part Stalin, mistrustful of anybody and everybody, including Hitler, was quite prepared to play along to buy time and see what developed.

It did not take long for the *Führer*'s next move to be made, and several uncomfortable provisions of the German–Russian pact to unfold. The German invasion of Poland began on 1 September 1939, quickly followed by declarations of war by Britain, France, Australia, and New Zealand. By 17 September the rapid advance of the *Wehrmacht* came to a halt, having overrun approximately half of Poland's territory. Then, as the world watched mesmerised, the Red Army rolled westward from its borders to occupy the other half. Not for the first time in its stormy history, Poland had ceased to exist as a nation. It was evident that some 'carving up' of territory had been agreed between the USSR and Germany, and more was to come. Included in the Soviet 'sphere of influence' were the Baltic republics of Lithuania, Latvia and Estonia, and also intended as a Soviet satellite was Finland.

The Finns, however, had other ideas. Resisting intense Soviet political pressure for two months, they finally felt obliged to mobilise their vastly outnumbered 200,000-strong army, whereupon Stalin broke off negotiations and on 31 November 1939, invaded. Despite having no armoured units and no heavy artillery, the Finnish forces not only held the mighty Red Army but in some areas threw it back in confusion; while in Berlin, Hitler noted with satisfaction the difficulties Russia had overcoming a substantially weaker enemy. The problems must have been equally apparent in the Kremlin, but, Stalin nevertheless ordered the assault pressed home until finally the Finns, after inflicting heavy losses on the Russians, were forced to ask for an armistice. This was refused, but considering their dominant position, the terms offered by the Russians, and accepted by the Finns on 13 March, were not as severe as they might have been. They also offer a fascinating insight into the Russian High Command's thinking, and have considerable bearing on later operations in the Barents Sea.

The Russians were to lease the Hanko Peninsula from Finland (for thirty years), giving them control over the entrance to the Gulf of Finland; they would also occupy Viipuri and the Karelian Isthmus, enabling them to defend Leningrad in depth. To the north Russia would control the mountains west of Kandalaksha, a strong defensive position covering the railway line from Murmansk on the Barents Sea coast to Leningrad and the Russian interior. It is apparent from these dispositions that the Soviet regime fully expected a war on its western frontier, and was also fully aware that Murmansk, and Archangel further east along the coast, were the only ports in western Russia capable of receiving supplies in any quantity.

Following Germany's invasion of Norway and Denmark in April 1940, events in western Europe developed at speed. On 10 May Winston Churchill replaced Neville Chamberlain as Prime Minister of Great Britain, while on the same day German troops invaded Belgium and the Netherlands. The *Blitzkrieg* swept on through France, forcing the evacuation of the British Expeditionary Force and a substantial number of its French allies from Dunkirk.

The German–Italian Axis now controlled all of western Europe with the exception of an area of southern France controlled by the Vichy regime (in effect a German puppet government) and Spain, neutral but pro-Fascist. A further expansion of the Axis powers was announced on 27 September when the Tripartite Pact between Germany, Italy, and Japan was made public.

Britain's European allies had been knocked out of the fight with devastating rapidity, and a substantial portion of the land forces avail-

2

able to her in the European theatre had only just escaped annihilation. Despite these hammer blows the British government and people, both strengthened by the unflinching resolve and stirring rhetoric of Prime Minister Churchill, determined that there would be no deals and no capitulation. Britain would remain without an ally with armies in the field against Germany until June 1941.

———

During the summer of 1940, the Battle of Britain and the RAF's defeat of the *Luftwaffe* brought Hitler's attention back to his principal obsession – Russia. The German navy would step up attacks on Britain's supply routes by U-boat and surface raiders, while the *Luftwaffe* switched from a direct confrontation with the RAF to bombing Britain's civilian population in her cities. In this way, it was hoped, Britain could be kept at arm's length until public morale cracked and she would be forced to sue for peace on German terms. In the meantime, the great mass of Germany's formidable military power would be unleashed on Russia.

At 1.35 a.m. on Sunday, 22 June 1941 Adolf Hitler launched Operation *Barbarossa*, the invasion of Russia. Having noted the difficulties which the Red Army experienced suppressing the troublesome Finns, Hitler's high command had no doubts as to the outcome; nevertheless preparations had been meticulous and the sheer scale of the German invasion was awesome. From the Baltic Sea in the north to the Black Sea in the south stood some 3,000,000 men, 3200 tanks, and 7500 guns. To the rear, stretching the full length of the front in a band 100 miles (161 km) wide, were the ammunition dumps, stores, fuel, half a million lorries, 600,000 horses, and all the accoutrements and paraphernalia necessary to support this vast array. Covering the invasion would be 775 bombers, 310 dive bombers, 830 single-engine fighters, 90 twin-engine fighters, 710 reconnaissance aircraft and, for operations in the Baltic and Black Sea, 55 seaplanes.[3]

Behind the invading armies came the SS *Einsatzgruppen*, the death squads, the butchers and executioners whose mission it was to obliterate any vestige of Bolshevism, and reduce the surviving Slav population to abject slavery. The Nazis' unholy war had begun.

Opposing this terrifying force the Red Army was, on paper, impressive; but there were serious, almost fatal, cracks in the edifice presented to the world. In theory at least, the Red Army had some 2,000,000 men, 20,000 tanks, and 12,000 aircraft[4] available in its western provinces to pit against the invaders. Many units, however, were substantially under strength, and there were worse problems. In the mid-1930s the Red Army could justly claim to be one of the finest fighting forces in the world. Noting this power, Joseph Stalin, with the obsessive paranoia of the absolute dictator, perceived threats and plots against him, and in 1937 unleashed the secret police, the NKVD, and as vicious as anything the Nazis had to offer, against the officer corps of the Red Army. Between 1937 and 1938 three of the five marshals of the USSR, eleven deputy commissars of defence, thirteen of fifteen army commanders, *all* the military district commanders and 35,000 officers of lower rank were executed, imprisoned, 'disappeared' or, for the fortunate few, merely dismissed. Only those officers who displayed total unquestioning obedience to Stalin remained. The war with Finland underlined the crippling effects of such blind reliance on 'higher authority' as officers at all levels made no attempt at individual enterprise or initiative, and instead simply waited for orders from above. Finally, sheer weight of numbers told against the Finns, but the Russians would not have that ace to play against the advancing hordes of the ruthlessly efficient, state-of-the-art German military machine.

To compound the problems, despite warnings from Britain and the United States, Stalin was convinced that Hitler would not break the non-aggression pact so soon after its inception. In order to reduce the possibility of border incidents and heightened tensions in the area, many of the Soviet 'advance' units were withdrawn miles behind their forward positions, in many instances scattered over wide areas with at best antiquated communications systems.

When the storm broke the Russian 'front' was swept away, and despite pockets of resistance German mechanised units along the whole line of advance sped deep into western Russia.

As the German invasion erupted into his country, Stalin bombarded the British government with urgent pleas for help for his hard-pressed armies. Although in its early stages the war in Russia did not appear destined to last long – so rapidly did the invaders gain ground – Churchill was painfully aware that Russia was the only ally Britain had with armies in the field against the mutual enemy, and it was vital to keep her in the fight. Despite severe shortages of supplies, equipment and ships of all kinds, especially escorts, the Prime Minister undertook to have regular convoys sent from Britain to the Russian Arctic ports of Murmansk and Archangel.

Relations between the British and Soviet governments were never going to be easy given the preceding years of mutual distrust, especially since it was widely known that Prime Minister Churchill was unshakeably anti-Communist, and while the revolution in Russia was under way had, as a senior government minister, publicly and unequivocally supported the White Russian (anti-Communist) forces. Given these feelings, when asked how he proposed to respond to the German invasion of Russia, Churchill firmly nailed his colours to the mast with his famous remark: 'If Hitler invaded Hell, I would at least give the Devil a favourable mention in the House of Commons'.[5]

Despite the best of intentions things got off to a shaky start. Prior to the German invasion, British intelligence, having broken the *Wehrmacht* Enigma code, became aware of the build-up of forces taking place on the Russian border. Churchill was keen to develop a 'one-to-one' relationship with Stalin and sent a personal warning of the German plans to the Soviet leader, with instructions to the British ambassador to Moscow, Sir Stafford Cripps, that he should hand it personally to Stalin. The Ambassador argued the point, believing that it should be sent 'through channels' via the appropriate Soviet government department. As a result of much to-ing and fro-ing the message did not reach Stalin for weeks, by which time much of its impact had been lost.[6]

By September 1941 it was all too obvious that the Russians were in serious trouble, and on the 4th of that month the Soviet ambassador to London, M. Maisky, passed on Stalin's urgent request for: 'a second front somewhere in the Balkans or France, capable of drawing away 30/40 [German] divisions, also, 30,000 tons of aluminium by the beginning of October, and monthly minimum of aid amounting to 400 aircraft and 500 tanks of small or medium size'.[7]

One week later Stalin telegraphed directly to Churchill: 'It seems to me that Great Britain could without risk land in Archangel 25/30 divisions, or transport them across Iran to the southern regions of the USSR.'[8]

As previously indicated, Churchill was only too aware of the need to support the Russians and keep them in the fight – without the Russian campaign Germany's full attention would be turned on Britain. The Prime Minister was, therefore, perfectly prepared to send all the supplies which could be managed, at times to the detriment of Britain's own needs; but he was not prepared to send British troops. In the ensuing weeks Russian requests for British divisions became more and more insistent, while Sir Stafford Cripps in Moscow, caught up in an atmosphere of crisis rapidly descending into catastrophe, bombarded the Foreign Office with messages relaying Russian 'disappointment' that no British troops would be sent, and warning of a possibly serious weakening of morale. The Soviets were obviously under intense pressure, but Churchill had problems of his own. Britain was still under heavy air attack; U-boats were waging a ferocious war against her transatlantic supply routes; food rationing was introduced, and her only campaign currently in operation against German forces, in North Africa, was not going well. Churchill's patience finally snapped and on 28 October 1941, via Foreign Secretary Anthony Eden, the Prime Minister despatched a cable to Sir Stafford Cripps outlining a few 'home truths':

1 The Russians brought the war on themselves when, by their pact with Ribbentrop [German Foreign Minister], they let Hitler loose on Poland.
2 The Russians cut themselves off from an effective second front when they refused to intervene in 1940 and allowed the French army to be destroyed.
3 If, prior to the German invasion, the Russians had consulted us, arrangements could have been made as regards munitions etc.
4 Instead until Hitler attacked, Britain did not know if the Russians would fight or whose side they would be on.
5 Britain was left alone for a year while every Communist in the country tried to hamper our war effort, on orders from Moscow.
6 If Britain had been invaded . . . or starved in the Battle of the Atlantic, the Soviet government would have remained utterly indifferent.
7 Despite warnings, Russia left Hitler to choose his moment and his enemies.
8 Russia was not short of manpower, what she needed was equipment, which Britain would endeavour to supply.[9]

Churchill was evidently 'letting off steam', and did not propose that Cripps should pass his comments on to the Russians verbatim, but he fully intended that the British ambassador should bear them in mind in his dealings with the Soviets.

Aware that the Royal Navy was already considerably stretched by escort duties in the Atlantic (despite invaluable assistance from the Royal Canadian Navy), plus substantial operations in the Mediterranean and the requirements of the Home Fleet, Churchill nevertheless insisted that the Admiralty make ships available to escort convoys to the Russian Arctic ports in the Barents Sea.

Concurrent with Operation *Barbarossa*, German troops entered the territory of their reluctant allies the Finns, and Russian foresight following the war with Finland with regard to their dispositions for protecting the ports of Murmansk and Archangel and the crucial rail link to the Russian interior, now became apparent.

A small exploratory convoy carrying mainly aircraft departed from Iceland on 21 August, and arrived in Russia without incident. A system of convoys was thereafter set in motion, commencing with *PQ1* which departed from Iceland on 28 September 1941, arriving at Archangel on 11 October – returning convoys (in ballast) were given the prefix *QP*. By the end of 1941, seven convoys had sailed through to Russia carrying vital supplies – 750 tanks, 800 fighters, 1400 vehicles, and over 100,000 tons (101,600 tonnes) of stores.

President Theodore Roosevelt believed that the United States should and would join the fight against Facism in Europe. However, in 1940 he faced re-election, making it necessary to court a vocal and not in-substantial 'isolationist' grouping in Congress and among the public at large. Nevertheless, the President ensured that supplies were sent to Britain and, in exchange for US rights to use bases in certain British possessions, arranged for the transfer to the Royal Navy of fifty old but still welcome US Navy destroyers. For Britain the first hope of the war came when Germany invaded Russia. The second came on Sunday, 8 December 1941, when Japanese forces attacked the US fleet at Pearl Harbor without warning – followed by Hitler's declaration of war on the United States in support of his Japanese allies. The German decla-ration neatly solved any problems which President Roosevelt might have had persuading the public that America's war lay across the Atlantic as well as the Pacific.

With the entrance of the United States into the war, plans were put in hand to increase transatlantic shipments so that supplies could be sent specifically for Russia and not taken from those sent for Britain's war effort, as had previously been the case.

It took the German high command some time to appreciate the importance of stopping the resupply of the Red Army through the Arctic ports. Possibly they did not believe that the campaign would last long enough for the convoys to matter; however, this would be only one of a number of reasons for the lack of German activity for several months of convoy traffic. From the opening of *Barbarossa* reconnaissance flights had been restricted as a result of aircraft being withdrawn from *Luftflotte* V (the German air fleet responsible for Norway) to assist with the campaign in Russia. Additionally, a principal cause must have been the German high command's lack of an effective inter-service general staff to co-ordinate the needs and responsibilities of the *Wehrmacht, Kriegsmarine* and *Luftwaffe*. On the contrary there was more often than not undisguised hostility between the heads of the different services, encouraged by Hitler on the principle of 'divide and rule'. This antipathy was particularly true of *Reichsmarschall* Hermann Goering, commander-in-chief (C-in-C) of the *Luftwaffe*, and Grand Admiral Erich Raeder, C-in-C *Kriegsmarine*, who had a long-running and furious argument over the control of naval aviation. This argument was never resolved, despite the conclusion of a pact in 1939, which Goering immediately proceeded to undermine by starving squadrons earmarked for the navy of aircraft. A similar dispute between the RAF and the Royal Navy lasted for over a decade between the wars, but was finally settled when naval air power (the Fleet Air Arm) was transferred to the control of the navy between 1937 and 1939. Goering, the former First World War fighter ace, proved to be a highly incompetent service chief, and to make matters worse appeared ready to do almost anything to flatter Hitler in an attempt to improve his own position to the detriment of the other service chiefs, whom he considered rivals to be fought as hard as the enemy. Such damaging rivalry did nothing to assist combined operations to hunt down Allied shipping.

To begin with Russia-bound convoys would consist of fifteen or so merchant ships, concentrated in north-west Scotland at Loch Ewe and/or Icelandic ports; however as the situation became more pressing, the number of ships increased to thirty or more. The escort would usually consist of a distant force of heavy ships from the Home Fleet comprising (dependent upon availability) a battleship or battle-cruiser, one or more heavy cruisers and a destroyer screen. An aircraft carrier should ideally have accompanied the heavy ships or the convoy itself to give air cover, but this was rarely possible due to the lack of carriers available to the fleet until the specifically designed escort carriers began to come on stream in 1943. The capital ships from the Home Fleet would operate some 300–400 miles* (552–742 km) from the convoy, but remain within high-speed striking distance in the hope of catching German surface raiders operating from northern

---

* From this point on 'miles' will refer to nautical miles, with the appropriate metric conversion, unless otherwise stated.

Norway. The British heavy ships would not, however, proceed east of Bear Island (see map A p. 144), as this would bring them within range of U-boats and the *Luftwaffe*. Secondly, there would be a detached covering force, usually two light cruisers, which would shadow the convoy through the Barents Sea, remaining at some 30–40 miles (55–75 km) distance, also to avoid U-boats. Close escort and anti-submarine protection would be provided by destroyers supported by an assorted force of corvettes, trawlers, minesweepers and occasionally, during summer months when the *Luftwaffe* was active, an anti-aircraft cruiser.

By 1942 Hitler was becoming convinced that the Allies planned an invasion of Norway, and to counter this threat and bolster attacks on the Arctic convoys he ordered a concentration of German capital ships in Norwegian waters. The battleship *Tirpitz* was subsequently located by British reconnaissance in Aas Fjord, 15 miles (27 km) from Trondheim, on 23 January 1942; while on 11 February the battle-cruisers *Scharnhorst* and *Gneisenau*, accompanied by the heavy cruiser *Prinz Eugen* and escorts, began their epic dash from Brest northward through the English Channel. British forces were slow to react and the ships got through undamaged by air and sea attacks; however *Gneisenau* hit a mine and *Scharnhorst* hit two. Both ships were able to proceed to German ports, where *Gneisenau* was further damaged by air attack while in dry dock at Kiel. *Prinz Eugen* continued on to Norway in company with the pocket battleship *Admiral Scheer*, and although the heavy cruiser was torpedo-damaged *en route*, a powerful German naval force was now building up.

In the meantime a further four convoys, *PQ8*, *9*, *10* and *11*, had by the last week of February delivered cargo from fifty-six merchantmen into Murmansk (Archangel being frozen during the Arctic winter), for the loss of one ship sunk, and one damaged but towed to the Kola Inlet (the entrance to Murmansk).

German actions against the convoys inevitably grew in intensity, and losses of both merchant and naval vessels in the Arctic began to mount, to the extent that the Admiralty proposed that sailings be suspended for the summer months, the period of perpetual Arctic daylight. Churchill, pressed by both Stalin and Roosevelt to increase not decrease shipments, vetoed the proposal. His memo of 17 May 1942 to General Sir Hastings Ismay, Chief of Staff to the Minister of Defence and liaison with the Chiefs of Staff Committee, explains the predicament:

1 Not only Premier Stalin but President Roosevelt will object very much to our desisting from running the convoys now. The Russians are in heavy action, and will expect us to run the risks and pay the price entailed by our contribution. The United States ships are queuing up. My own feeling, mingled with much anxiety, is that the convoy ought to sail on the 18th [of May]. The operation is justified if a half get through. The failure on our part to make the attempt would weaken our influence with both our major allies. I share your misgivings but I feel it is a matter of duty.

2 I presume all the ships are armed with AA guns and that not more than 25 would be sent.

3 I will bring the question before the Cabinet tomorrow (Monday) in your presence, but meanwhile all preparations should proceed.[10]

The convoy in question, *PQ16*, consisting of thirty-five merchant ships, subsequently sailed on 21 May and on 27 May was subjected to attacks by 108 torpedo bombers. These attacks continued for five days, but losses were kept down to six ships. Churchill had in some measure trusted to luck and that luck had held; however it was about to run out.

On Finnish and Norwegian airfields around the North Cape, the northernmost tip of Norway, the *Luftwaffe* assembled a formidable force of torpedo bombers, dive bombers, level bombers and fighter support. In addition Admiral Doenitz, C-in-C of the U-boat arm of the *Kriegsmarine*, received orders to increase the number of operational units in the Arctic to ten.

As all available Allied escorts were required for Operation *Harpoon*, a convoy for the relief of hard-pressed Malta, the next Russia convoy, *PQ17*, was scheduled for the end of June.

The Admiralty in general, and C-in-C Home Fleet Admiral Tovey in particular, were very well aware that running convoys through to Arctic Russia in the summer months of perpetual daylight would incur substantial risk of heavy loss in merchant and escort vessels and their crews. The chances of discovery by U-boats or round-the-clock *Luftwaffe* reconnaissance would be virtually certain.

Up to this point the German high command had used only U-boats and air attack against convoys, but Admiral Tovey and Admiral of the Fleet Sir Dudley Pound were convinced that surface raiders would also be brought into action, including the battleship *Tirpitz*. The upper echelons of Naval High Command had a wary respect for this powerful adversary, fearing disaster should she ever get loose. In conversations between the two men Sir Dudley Pound advised Admiral Tovey that if *Tirpitz* were to break out of her Norwegian base to intercept a convoy, he might well order it to scatter. Tovey was not in agreement with this approach, believing that nothing would be gained as the merchantmen would then be isolated and picked off at will by U-boat and aircraft attack. Keeping the convoy together, he maintained, would at least give the close escort some chance of harassing and delaying the attackers until British capital ships could be brought into action in support.

Convoy *PQ17* comprised thirty-five merchantmen, and sailed on 27 June 1942 from the Icelandic port of Hvalfjord. Covering the passage to Russia, a powerful escort included with the Home Fleet distant-covering force the aircraft carrier HMS *Victorious*, and for the first time ships of the US Navy accompanying both the Home Fleet units and the detached cruiser force in the Barents Sea.

Also very aware of the improved prospects for attacking Russia-bound convoys which summer provided, Grand Admiral Erich Raeder fully intended to combine operations by *Tirpitz* and the German battle group in Norway with attacks by U-boats and the *Luftwaffe*. However, he also had his problems, not least of which was Hitler's extreme reluctance to put his heavy ships at risk. Hitler insisted that before convoys were attacked by major German surface units, any British aircraft carriers with the supporting forces were to be attacked and destroyed by the *Luftwaffe*. This placed an impossible handicap on the German naval high command, and was compounded by the *Führer's* orders that no attacks were to be made by any German heavy ships unless he personally gave the order for them to sail.[11] In an attempt to comply with these crippling restrictions, Raeder devised Operation *Rosselsprung* ('Knight's Move'), which was to be carried out in two phases. Upon detection of a convoy the German heavy ships were to sail from their bases along the Norwegian coast to concentrate at sortie ports in northern Norway, there to await Hitler's final sanction for an offensive operation. This movement in advance of final attack orders would have a completely unforeseen outcome.

PQ17 first made contact with enemy forces on 1 July, when escorting destroyers attacked two German U-boats which were discovered on the surface. The U-boats dived unharmed but later that day a reconnaissance aircraft circled the convoy, followed by the first of a number of aircraft attacks, which continued for several days. Losses were suffered but for the most part these attacks were successfully beaten off.

Putting *Rosselsprung* into action, Raeder ordered *Tirpitz* and *Admiral Hipper* north from Trondheim, and *Admiral Scheer* and *Lützow* north from Narvik, all bound for Altenfjord. *Lützow* grounded, but *Tirpitz, Hipper*, and *Scheer* arrived at their destination on 3 July; on that afternoon British aircraft reconnaissance reported *Tirpitz* and *Hipper* missing from Trondheim.

On receiving this report, Admiral of the Fleet Sir Dudley Pound became concerned that *Tirpitz* was out and heading for *PQ17*; his apprehension mounted during the ensuing hours as no confirmation of *Tirpitz*'s whereabouts was received. As the hours passed Ultra[12] decrypts of German radio traffic pointed towards a concentration of heavy ships, probably including *Tirpitz*, at Altenfjord, but gave no indication that a battle group was at sea bound for the convoy; nor did the standard warnings to U-boats in the area materialise, advising them to be on the lookout for approaching friendly surface units. Despite the lack of supporting evidence, Admiral Pound's conviction grew that *Tirpitz* was on her way to intercept *PQ17* and, by-passing Admiral Tovey (who was at sea with the Home Fleet distant covering force), despatched three signals direct to the convoy escort which would have disastrous results. The first of these reached Rear-Admiral Hamilton, in command of the accompanying cruiser squadron, at approximately 21.20 on 4 July and read: 'Most Immediate. Cruiser force to withdraw westward at high speed. (2111B/4).'

This first message, despatched as a result of reported U-boat activity in the area, was followed in quick succession by two further urgent transmissions, the first arriving with Rear-Admiral Hamilton at approximately 22.00: 'Immediate. Owing to threat from surface ships, convoy is to disperse and proceed to Russian ports. (2123B/4).' And finally: 'Most immediate. My 2123/4, convoy is to scatter. (2136/4).[13]

Rear-Admiral Hamilton's understanding (and that of the other senior officers of the escort) was that a 'convoy is to scatter' signal would only be sent if the Admiralty had definite information that an attack by powerful surface ships was imminent. As a consequence he expected to see *Tirpitz* and a battle group steaming over the horizon at any moment. The 'scatter' signal was passed to the convoy at 22.15, followed by much disbelief, repeats and confirmations. Finally the port columns of merchant ships peeled slowly off to the left, starboard columns to the right, while the centre columns carried straight on.

Rear-Admiral Hamilton ordered the destroyer escort to close on his cruisers and at 22.30 the combined force turned westward, steering to pass south of the dispersing merchant ships (i.e. between the merchantmen and the supposed German surface units). As ordered, the remainder of the close escort also 'scattered', leaving the merchantmen to their fate. Only one of the escorts continued to offer any protection, the trawler *Ayreshire* succeeding in shepherding three freighters as far as Novaya Zemlya by 10 July.

His orders being unequivocal, Hamilton kept on westward at 25 knots, keeping the destroyers with him, reasoning that when the convoy scattered the enemy would attack it with U-boats and aircraft, and send their surface units after him. This being the case, he might be able to draw them onto *Victorious*'s aircraft and possibly the Home Fleet battle group itself.[14]

In the Barents Sea the situation in which the defenceless merchant ships found themselves quickly descended into tragedy. On 5 July six vessels were sunk by air attack and six torpedoed by U-boats. One ship was bombed on the 6th, and between the evening of the 6th and the early morning of the 8th four more were torpedoed. Two more were sunk on the night of the 9th/10th.[15]

As for *Tirpitz*, Hitler's permission to launch an attack by the battle group was finally obtained on the forenoon of 5 July, and the executive order to proceed to sea given at 11.37, by which time Hamilton's cruiser force was known to be heading westward, and Admiral Tovey's covering force to be some 450 miles (832 km) from the convoy and the North Cape alike. During the day German intelligence intercepted messages from Allied ships from which it was calculated that Admiral Tovey's battle group would be able to close sufficiently to launch an air attack by 01.00 on the 6th. As reports of the many sinkings by U-boat and air attack came through, it became apparent that sending the battle group after the stragglers was simply not worth the risk. Consequently at 21.32 on the 5th *Tirpitz* and her consorts were ordered to abandon the operation and twenty minutes later altered course for Altenfjord.[16] The German battleship had delivered a major victory without having fired a shot.

The final tally was thirteen ships destroyed by air attack, and ten sunk by submarines, for the loss of six German aircraft. Quite apart from the priceless loss of life (153 merchant seamen lost their lives), the Red Army was deprived of 430 tanks, 210 aircraft and 3350 vehicles,[17] equivalent to the destruction which might be expected from a major land battle.

The tactical problem of fighting a convoy through against a

powerful surface battle group plus U-boats and aircraft was a difficult one. The standard tactic for defence of a convoy against powerful surface units was to scatter, but for fighting off U-boat or aircraft attack the best defence was to remain together. As I have mentioned, Admiral Tovey was not in agreement with the 'scatter' approach even in the event of attack by *Tirpitz*. One reason may be the belief held by some that the Barents Sea gave too little room for the effective dispersal of a large convoy. Had the convoy not scattered, *Tirpitz* and consorts would certainly have attacked, no doubt causing substantial losses. Probably the only safe, but temporary, alternative at the time *Tirpitz* was discovered to have left her home port was to reverse the convoy's course and await developments, perhaps trying to draw the German surface units after the merchant ships onto *Victorious*'s aircraft or the Home Fleet battle group – much as Rear-Admiral Hamilton had hoped to do with his cruisers. However, given Hitler's paranoia concerning damage to his heavy ships (a factor unknown to the Allies), it is doubtful that he would have sanctioned a chase far enough to the west for this to have been possible – and at some point the convoy *had* to be fought through, one way or another. Admiral of the Fleet Sir Dudley Pound found himself confronted by several extremely difficult options, but it is reasonable to suggest that instead of issuing peremptory orders he might have been better advised to keep Tovey and Hamilton apprised of precisely what was known of enemy surface ship movements, and leave decisions on the best course of action to the officers on the spot. Rear-Admiral Hamilton alone knew the prevailing weather conditions, which during the course of the voyage varied from very good visibility to thick fog, flat calm to full gale, and was in the best position to evaluate the prospects for evasion or defence. It has been suggested that a contributing factor to Sir Dudley Pound's decision may have been the inclusion of US Navy ships with the escort, and the repercussions which might ensue should one or more of them be sunk while under British command. This may have been a factor, but what must be said is that those who have never had to hold such a post at such a time, can only guess at the pressure and stress which must be endured.

Pressure and stress were also getting to the political leadership. Winston Churchill now had to try to explain the loss of so much valuable *matériel* to Stalin, against a background of complicated and mistrustful relations with the Soviet Union. Despite pacts and public reassurances of mutual support by and between the three principal allies in the European war, Churchill and Roosevelt feared that if Russia's horrendous losses continued to mount Stalin might conclude a separate peace with Hitler. At the same time Stalin entertained suspicions that Britain and the United States might change sides and join Germany's war against Russia; there being, after all, no enthusiasm for Bolshevism whatsoever in the governments of the Western democracies.

Churchill tried to soften the twin blows of the fate of *PQ17* and the resultant cancellation of the next summer convoy, *PQ18*, by alluding to the build-up of troops for a second front (for which Stalin had long been pressing). Stalin, however, had German armies racing across his country and was in no mood to be mollified.

To escape the advancing Germans, most Soviet government departments were sent eastwards to Kuibyshev. Stalin, however, remained in Moscow, which was where Winston Churchill visited him in August. Churchill was subjected to another lambasting over *PQ17* and made acutely aware of the seriousness of the military position. On his return to London the British prime minister, convinced that a convoy should be pushed through to Murmansk in September to maintain vital Anglo-Russian cooperation, notified the Admiralty that despite their sound military reasoning against a further summer enterprise, a convoy and escort should be assembled and despatched at the earliest possible opportunity.

PQ18 sailed from Loch Ewe on 2 September 1942, and consisted of thirty-nine merchant ships joined by a further six in Iceland. Escorting this convoy, something of an armada had been assembled by the Admiralty. By drawing warships away from other duties a Home Fleet battle group comprising two battleships, a cruiser and four destroyers maintained position to the north-west of Jan Mayen Island, while from Western Approaches Command six destroyers and five trawlers accompanied the convoy as far as Iceland. Taking the convoy on to Murmansk the close escort comprised two anti-aircraft ships, two destroyers, four corvettes, three minesweepers and four trawlers. An additional fighting destroyer escort of sixteen ships plus a light cruiser joined two days out from Iceland, and for the first time an escort aircraft carrier accompanied an Arctic convoy into the Barents Sea, itself escorted by two further destroyers. Also in the area were three cruisers supporting homebound convoy *QP14*, and two cruisers and a destroyer operating a regular relief trip for the garrison at Spitzbergen. Covering the convoy's southern flank and on the lookout for German surface units operating from northern Norway were up to ten

15

submarines. Determined to keep tight control of the situation and in close touch with the Admiralty to avoid any chance of a repetition of the *PQ17* débâcle, Admiral Tovey remained at Scapa Flow while his Home Fleet second-in-command, Vice-Admiral Sir Bruce Fraser, took command at sea.

Those in the *Kriegsmarine* and *Luftwaffe* who should have put two and two together appear not to have realised that their success against *PQ17* had been the result of an unintentional combined operation between surface ships, U-boats and aircraft. The consequence of this, and Hitler's reluctance to commit his big ships, was that attacks on *PQ18* were left to U-boats and the *Luftwaffe*. Commencing on 13 September and lasting nine days, a stream of ferocious attacks was launched against the convoy. Thirteen of the forty-five merchant ships were lost, at a cost to the *Luftwaffe* of forty-one aircraft, and three priceless U-boats to the *Kriegsmarine*. Following the *PQ17* débâcle, fighting thirty-two ships through was a considerable relief to the Allies, but the loss of thirteen was a substantial price to pay; and the huge escort required put a severe strain on the Royal Navy, particularly in the number of destroyers required. Also caught up in the attacks, the homeward-bound convoy *QP14* lost three merchant ships out of fifteen, plus a destroyer, a minesweeper, and an oiler.

Almost from the moment Germany invaded Russia, Stalin had pressed for a second front in Europe. This proved impractical in the early stages, but Churchill and Roosevelt did agree on Operation *Torch*, an Anglo-American landing in North Africa. *Torch* drew all available escorts from convoy and other duties, and warship cover for the Atlantic convoys was so weakened that losses increased sharply. Churchill again faced the prospect of having to advise Stalin that convoys to Russia would have to be cancelled, in all probability until January 1943.

He attempted to obtain escort reinforcement in the shape of twelve US destroyers, but Roosevelt had to decline owing to the requirements of *Torch* and other commitments. The Admiralty also hoped that ships might be obtained from the Mediterranean to escort a Russia convoy, but instead of giving them up, Admiral Cunningham, C-in-C Mediterranean, asked for more. The problem was outlined by the Admiralty in a minute to the Prime Minister dated 22 November 1942, which stated essentially that:

- The situation in the North Atlantic is severe and cannot be allowed to continue. The Minister of War Transport fears that if convoys continue to be knocked about in the Atlantic as at present the signs are that merchant seamen may refuse to sail.
- Long-range aircraft for the Atlantic have been approved but it will be some time before they are operational, also weather conditions greatly reduce the number of days on which they can operate.
- Proposals made to the United States and Canada to temporarily augment escorts over the western portion [of the Atlantic] mid-voyage have been agreed, although this weakens their escorts on the run west of Newfoundland and would have to be cancelled if U-boats return in strength.
- To deal with the eastern portion of the mid voyage [not covered by air support], we must provide two reinforcing groups. One can be scraped together from ships returning from 'Torch', and it may be possible to obtain US agreement to releasing British ships working on the convoy route from Guantanamo to New York.
- Convoy *PQ19* can be run on 22 December by reducing the destroyer escort from sixteen to seven but this may necessitate cruisers going right through [to Russia] with the convoy. Admiral of The Fleet does not like substitution of cruisers for destroyers, but sees no alternative.
- We have previously agreed with the USSR to run three convoys every two months. This is now out of the question, and the best possible is one convoy every thirty-three days. This will cause severe strain on Home Fleet destroyers.
- The USSR may not be able to accept more than one thirty-ship convoy every thirty-three days as they have only twelve unloading berths and each ship takes ten to twelve days to unload. There is also some doubt as to whether the Russian railways can handle even one thirty-ship convoy every thirty-three days.[18]

With the battles along the Russian front, and at Stalingrad in particular, consuming men and *matériel* at a relentlessly escalating rate, Soviet insistence on further convoys reached a new intensity. It is worth bearing in mind that on top of all the military difficulties to be overcome, by the end of 1942 Britain was desperately short of food and raw materials herself. To take an example, only 300,000 tons (304,800 tonnes) of commercial bunker fuel for civilian use was to be had in the country, and this was used at a rate of 130,000 tons (132,080 tonnes) per month.[19] Nevertheless, Churchill realised that regardless of all difficulties, it was again necessary to 'stand the hazard of the die', and on 24 November cabled Stalin advising:

17

- Although US President unable to lend twelve destroyers have made arrangements for convoy over thirty ships to sail from Iceland 22 December. Germans have moved bulk of aircraft from North Norway to Southern Europe to counter 'Torch'. German surface forces in Norway still on guard.
- Shipping is limiting factor. To do 'Torch' we had to cut transatlantic escorts so fine that first half of November was worst month so far. UK and US budgeted to lose 700,000 tons per month and still improve margin. Over the year average losses are not quite so bad, but first fortnight in November was worse.[20]

Given the task of arranging the defence of the convoy Admiral Tovey proposed a change from the usual method to take into account, and take advantage of, the Arctic winter:

From late November to mid January the lack of daylight is such that air reconnaissance in the Arctic is virtually impossible. Provided that a convoy is of such a size that it can be handled and kept together, it therefore stands an excellent chance of evading both U-boat and surface attack and even of completing the passage without the enemy's knowing of its existence. A large convoy, on the other hand, is likely to fail to keep company, and to split (as did *QP15*) into a large number of small groups, covering a vast area and unaware of each other's position or composition. Such small groups would be more liable to detection by U-boats than a single concentrated convoy and would present the enemy surface forces with an ideal opportunity for an offensive sweep. Our own covering forces are always handicapped by having to identify a contact before they are free to attack; the enemy need not do so. The splitting of the convoy into a large number of scattered units would greatly add to this handicap.[21]

The Admiral's contention that greater control could be exercised over smaller convoys was accepted and it was decided that the thirty-ship convoy for December would be run in two fifteen-ship sections. It was also decided to drop the *PQ* prefix in favour of *JW*; while for return convoys *RA* replaced *QP*.

From the last quarter of 1941, the supply of fuel oil for the German navy had been critical. By April 1942 deliveries from Romania had fallen from 46,000 tons (46,736 tonnes) to 8000 tons (8128 tonnes) per month, and this was promised to the Italians for their campaign to keep the Mediterranean open to Axis shipping.[22] Such shortages did not, however, affect the submarines or pocket battleships, which burned diesel oil – still in comparatively plentiful supply. On the afternoon of 19 November 1942, at one of his regular meetings with Hitler, Grand Admiral Raeder again drew the *Führer*'s attention to the problem and received orders to return *Lützow* to Norway in view of her diesel-burning engines. Raeder also primed Hitler for the use of surface units by pointing out that while there were presently twenty-three submarines assigned to the Arctic, of which ten were in operational zones, during the months of almost perpetual night, submarine operations would be much less effective due to the absence of aerial reconnaissance and adverse weather conditions.[23] On the surface, with good visibility a U-boat could spot a convoy's smoke 30–40 miles (55–74 km), away, while in bad visibility prospects for making contact would be cut to 20 miles (37 km) with the use of hydrophones.[24] Second World War submarines could spend a comparatively limited time submerged owing to the need to recharge batteries and replenish their oxygen supply, a significant problem in the storms and blizzards of the Arctic winter. As a result of these considerations, and the fact that in the early years of the war detection equipment could only identify a submarine under water, the U-boats' favoured method of attack was at night on the surface. This approach was not best suited to the violent weather of the Arctic winter.

Raeder followed up his intention to use surface vessels by authorising Admiral Commanding Cruisers, Vice-Admiral Oskar Kummetz, to devise a plan to be put into action at the next opportunity.

While the political leadership and the generals and admirals conducted their grand strategy, for the men of all sides who fought in the Arctic there were two enemies – their human foe, and the weather. Often the latter would prove to be the more unforgiving, an enemy not only uncomfortable and inconvenient but packing a heavy punch.

1   Toland, John (1997) *Hitler*, Wordsworth Editions.
2   Ibid.
3   Pitt, Barrie & Francis (1998) *The Chronological Atlas of W.W.II*, Bookmart Edition.
4   Ibid.
5   Pelling, Henry (1999) *Winston Churchill*, Wordsworth Editions.
6   PRO. PREM 3/395.
7   Ibid.
8   Ibid.
9   Ibid.
10 PRO. PREM 3/393
11 PRO. ADM 234/369
12 The name given to decodes of German radio traffic, sent by operators using the Enigma coding machine. Believed by the Germans to be unbreakable, but cracked by British codebreakers at Bletchley Park. The German *B dienst* teams performed a similar service and had successes against British naval codes.
13 PRO. ADM 234/340
14 PRO. ADM 234/369
15 PRO. ADM 234/340
16 PRO. ADM 234/369
17 Ibid.
18 Ibid.
19 Watts, Anthony J. (1999) *The Royal Navy, An Illustrated History*, Brockhampton Press.
20 PRO. PREM 3/393
21 PRO. ADM 234/369
22 Ibid.
23 PRO. ADM 116/5307
24 AHB/II/117/3(B), p.270–1, quoted in Terraine, John (1997) *The Right of the Line*, Wordsworth Editions.

CHAPTER 2

COLD COMFORT

'What was life like in the Arctic in destroyers?' I asked Lieutenant-Commander John Patrick 'Paddy' Donovan, MBE, RN.

'Bloody!' was his pithy comment.

Paddy Donovan was born in Weymouth, Dorset, in 1919, into a naval family – both grandfathers had been in the Navy, as had his father and three uncles. During the Second World War his elder sister Kathleen became a WREN petty officer and his younger brother Tim also followed him into the ranks, but tragically went down with the battlecruiser *Repulse* in December 1941. His elder brother Mick had also been earmarked for the senior service but he was thrown from a horse while helping the local milk lady, and the accident affected his sight and hearing. Only one other Donovan seems to have been able to resist the siren call of the Navy – younger sister Connie became a WAAF mechanic.

Paddy Donovan saw service in battleships in the 1930s, and the cruiser *Norfolk* during the Abyssinian crisis of 1939, and survived the loss of the fast minelayer *Latona* in 1941, bombed and sunk while attempting to run supplies into besieged Tobruk. In the latter part of 1942 the then Second Lieutenant Donovan joined the new Royal Navy destroyer *Obedient* as gunnery officer. One of the first of the Navy's new class of escort destroyers, the ship was assigned to Arctic convoy protection, and Paddy needed to acclimatise himself quickly to the particular difficulties and dangers of serving in those far northern latitudes.

The waters of the Barents Sea need to be treated with utmost respect in peacetime, let alone in war. Sub-zero winds blast off the polar ice cap at up to hurricane strength, catching and freezing spray and rain, blowing it like shrapnel against a ship's upper works to set as layer upon layer of ice. This ice must be regularly chipped or steam-hosed away if the weight is not to cause stability problems and the serious risk of foundering. Ships take waves 70 ft (21.3 m) high 'green' over their decks, while in the depths of winter temperatures might register 50 degrees Celsius of frost. Any crewman unwise enough to go on deck in these conditions without gloves would find the flesh of his hand instantly 'welded' to metal by frost, should he touch it. On 17 January 1942 the escort destroyer *Matabele* was torpedoed in these treacherous waters and sank. A rescue vessel arrived on the scene in minutes but found only two survivors, the rest of the crew having frozen to death. To add to the difficulties, the warmer waters of the Gulf Stream enter the freezing Arctic, causing banks of thick fog to drift across the area, and the phenomenon known as 'layering' (different layers of warm and cold water), which was little understood at the time, but which seriously disrupted ASDIC* searches for submarines.

The polar ice edge fluctuates greatly with the changing seasons, and in winter it would come down far enough to force the convoys south of Bear Island, and consequently closer to German naval and air bases in northern Norway. Depending upon where the ice edge was situated, the arduous voyage from the UK to Russia would be from 1500 to 2000 miles (2760 to 3680 km). Winter would also see the freezing up of Archangel, leaving only Murmansk through which to discharge cargoes.

The Kola Inlet runs approximately north and south from the Barents Sea to Murmansk, and is the estuary for the River Tuloma (see map p. 23). On the western shore of the inlet some 5½ statute miles (8.85 km) from its mouth lies Polyarnoe, where destroyers and submarines were based, and where the C-in-C of the Russian Northern Fleet and the Senior British Naval Officer, North Russia, had their administrative offices. Across the inlet (8½ statute miles/13.7 km by water), lies Vaenga where the Royal Navy had established an auxiliary hospital with beds for seventy-four patients. Vaenga was connected by a single track railway with Murmansk, some 16 statute miles (25.7 km) to the south.

Murmansk lies along the eastern shore of the inlet, and since 1928 had been the subject of an ambitious expansion plan to develop what had been principally a fishing village into the Soviet Union's main ice-free northern port. During the war years the town was subjected to savage and sustained bombing attacks from the nearby *Luftwaffe* bases in Finland and Norway.[1]

Life aboard ship was miserable in the 'work horses' of convoy escort – destroyers, corvettes, minesweepers, trawlers and the like. A ship at sea works, in twenty-first century internet parlance, 24/7 or twenty-four hours a day, seven days a week. For the day-to-day business of convoy escort, a destroyer crew would be organised into four 'watches'

---

* Anti-submarine detection equipment developed between the wars by the Anglo-French Allied Submarine Detection Investigation Committee.

of four hours each, except for the dog watches which would be two hours – 4–6 p.m. and 6–8 p.m. This ensured that each watch rotated its time and took a turn at the unpopular 'graveyard shift', midnight to 4 a.m. Each watch had an officer plus four lookouts on the bridge, one lookout to each corner, while other members of the watch performed routine but essential tasks, which in the Arctic usually entailed using chipping hammers in the constant battle to prevent ice build up on the upper works. Guns would be unmanned but rotated at frequent intervals in an effort to prevent them freezing up.[2] Off watch below, things were not much better. Officers had cabins aft, except the captain, whose sea cabin would be below the bridge, enabling him to be called up at short notice. The men slept (or tried to) in hammocks slung in the mess decks. The atmosphere below would be warm, but fetid with stale sweat and damp clothing; steel doors banged to and fro as crew members working the ship came and went, while in heavy weather icy seas crashed over the ship and down companionways to the decks below. With little or no time to clean up, this would soon turn into a rancid greasy soup 2 or 3 inches (5–7 cm) deep, slopping about the deck. This, and bulkheads streaming with condensation, made keeping anything dry impossible.

Unlike larger ships, the turrets of Royal Navy destroyers were not enclosed; they comprised the gun and a partly enveloping shield. This would cause more problems in the freezing conditions, as ice would form not only on the barrels of the guns but also on breeches and other mechanisms. Anti-freeze grease would help, but would not completely eliminate the problem. If ice did form, the heat of the gun firing would

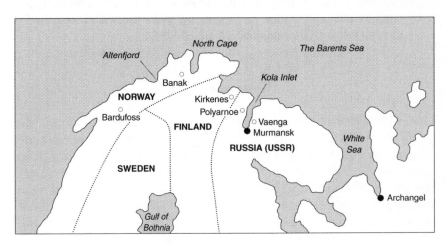

Northern Norway and the Kola Inlet

cause it to melt, and water might well seep into the breech, causing the gun to jam.[3]

Destroyers did not use Murmansk when they were in Russia, but were based with the submarines at Polyarnoe, just inside the Kola Inlet. A 'run ashore' for a little rest and relaxation was another pipe dream, as Paddy Donovan recalled.

'What recreation was there ashore?' I asked him.

'None at all. Except the Russian Officers' Club.

'What recreation was there at the Russian Officers' Club?'

'None at all!'[4]

There might have been nothing ashore, but the trip could be eventful. London-born Captain Michael Hutton, OBE, RN, then a seventeen-year-old midshipman fresh from Dartmouth Naval College, on his first posting to the new Fiji class cruiser HMS *Jamaica*, remembered an incident during Christmas 1942. With the ship at anchor off Murmansk he was midshipman of a ship's boat, and having ferried a sailor with appendicitis to the small hospital ashore on Christmas Day, a further trip was necessary the following day:

> Another quick trip ashore in the boat on Boxing Day and a real pleasure to hand round my cigarette case to Russian soldiers. On the return trip another important lesson was confirmed. Never, never, wear sea boots (wellies) as boat's crew. I had not spotted my bow man was an offender and he slipped overboard. His boots filled up and within seconds in that freezing water he was in real trouble and I knew he could not last for long. Probably within a minute we had him back onboard, just alive, and later I was pleased on behalf of myself and crew to be congratulated on our seamanship. As soon as the lucky sailor had recovered, I insisted he go all the way to Captain's Report.
>
> Good old Naval justice . . . the lesson had been driven home.[5]

Given the years of brainwashing by the Communist regime and the resultant frostiness of the local population as well as the climate, Murmansk and Archangel were not the most popular ports of call for naval or merchant seamen. Most sailors would certainly have echoed the words of one young Jamaican merchant seaman (a world away from his Caribbean home in both temperature and temperament) who, when asked for his thoughts on North Russia, replied, 'I'd sho' like to go any place else – jes' any place a-tall'.[6]

It would be wrong to suggest, however, that the Russians were completely unappreciative of the Allies' efforts. Mentioned in Dispatches for his part in the Barents Sea action, Paddy Donovan was also awarded the Russian Order of Patriotic War. This order came with a monthly payment, calculated in roubles, which his bank manager advised equated to around 7 shillings (35 p) per month. Some twenty months later, with *Obedient* in home waters and his wife Enid expecting a baby, it seemed to Paddy that the £7 or so which had accumulated would come in handy so off he went to the Russian embassy in London to collect. Finally a staff member handed over a large envelope which Paddy took to a nearby park to investigate. On examination it turned out to contain £77 – a pleasant surprise in the circumstances. His comments on his bank manager's arithmetic are not recorded!

It might be assumed that life aboard the larger ships would be easier, but this was not necessarily the case. As a seventeen-year old Boy 1st Class, Lieutenant-Commander Albert Twiddy, DSC, RN, had his first seagoing posting to the Southampton class cruiser HMS *Sheffield*, joining in July 1942. He recalled life on board.

What I did know at the time was that the ship was to be employed in Northern waters, and I was to get used to my new surroundings, new experiences of living with so many others . . . of confined living quarters well below decks, and the complete lack of any privacy whatsoever, at whatever the time of day or night. Furthermore, I had not appreciated that in just a few weeks' time I would find myself suffering extreme distress from seasickness, that the ship would be pressing its way through ice slush and frozen fog, and my messdeck quarters [would be] streaming with condensation, or iced up, with continuous mopping up to prevent water swilling around . . .

My duty tasks at sea involved lookout duties on the Bridge and Air Defence position for 8 hours in every 24, and a further 4 to 6 hours on general maintenance tasks, mostly spent chipping ice from the guns and upper decks when we were well into the Arctic Circle . . . Long Johns and duffel coats were the extent of our special warm clothing, though for bridge duties we were loaned a sheepskin coat which was passed onto our relief when he turned up to take over duty, as we had insufficient coats to be provided with one each. Balaclavas of course were an absolute essential, and parcels from home and some voluntary organisations provided us with these, together with woollen gloves and scarves. Of course we normally slept in hammocks, but under certain states of readiness for action we were required to sleep at or very near our action station. This, in my case, meant trying to sleep fully clothed on the steel deck of 'A' turret* where my action station was . . . It was almost a relief to pass into the Arctic Circle where we were freed from the constant dripping of condensation and of mopping it up, by virtue of the fact that the condensation simply froze, and remained to be chipped off from time to time.[7]

The weather was a powerful opponent, and it was not only the small, lightly built destroyers that were at risk. Paddy Donovan described an occurrence in February 1943 which illustrates the dangers:

We were going up to join a convoy . . . when the *Sheffield* went past us. We were in a heavy gale and the destroyers were slowed right down, but the cruiser was able to get past us. Two hours later we caught up and passed her . . . we could see 'A' turret, the whole of the lid was peeled right back . . . by weight of water.[8]

The incident also created a lasting impression in the mind of Boy 1st Class Albert Twiddy – he was in *Sheffield*'s 'A' turret at the time.

The voyage to Iceland . . . encountered violent storms and monstrous seas, so much so that the ship had to heave to in order to ride it out. There was considerable damage around the upper decks. The whalers at the davits were completely destroyed, and some ladders smashed away. It was almost impossible to go on deck and any necessary move-ment could only be made by hanging on to lifelines rigged throughout the open spaces. It was chaotic below decks, water swilling around the messdecks and flats, and reeking with the vomit that even the hardiest sailors fell victim to. Generally one felt safest when closed up at action stations, and I think that, for most of the time during this appalling weather, was where I was required to be. I was certainly closed up in 'A' turret on the forenoon when the heaviest of waves struck.

For any degree of comfort it was a matter of wedging oneself into position and staying there. The noise of the bows crashing into the oncoming seas, the rattle of anchor cables and other objects being moved around was a constant source of deafening noise and dis-comfort, but I cannot recall being alarmed for my own safety, the ship was so big and well built . . . but then I had never experienced such extreme conditions before. I could not see the sea, I could only feel its effect on me and the others around me. Solid food or even the thought of it was out of the question and 'Kye' [thick cocoa] was the only

---

* See Royal Navy turret designations, diagram HMS *Sheffield*, p. 128.

warming sustenance available if it survived the journey from the galley. I can readily recall that mid-morning, someone had managed to get some and that it was being dispensed into mugs when there was an almighty crash and a sudden flash of light, like lightning, then water cascading down upon us as we saw that one third of the [armoured] turret roof had disappeared and we were exposed to the violent sky and tons of foaming water breaking over the bow forcing its way into what had been just a few moments earlier, our watertight gun turret. Our immediate thoughts were that we had been attacked and struck by the gunfire from an unseen enemy, but apart from being shaken there were few physical injuries . . . Each successive wave poured more water in, which was swilling its way down into the lower areas of the turret.

Having informed the control tower of our plight, we were shortly ordered to evacuate the turret. It was of course impossible to get out on deck, and there was just one vertical ladder immediately below my telephone position so I was in the prime position to get out first. However, the hood of my duffel coat got caught up on a hook, and I was left virtually hanging over the only escape route. Strong hands soon lifted me clear and I got to the bottom faster than intended. This all seemed to happen so quickly . . . [but] the personnel in the handling rooms below quickly opened the watertight door leading us out to the lower deck. [We] were confronted by the damage control operator, who on being told that the turret was flooding, immediately closed the door again and put on all the watertight clips, effectively locking us all in. It was only after he had made his report and sought further instructions that we were released from the confines of the turret, but no escape from the water which had flooded a great part of the fore end of the ship.[9]

The daily round of a sailor's life when not on escort duty consisted of all the routine tasks of a shipboard existence, and as '. . . there were no ENSA comedians or dancing girls in North Russia',[10] the men had to make their own entertainment. Concert parties would be arranged and acts would volunteer or be shanghaied into doing a 'turn'. Paddy Donovan remembered that with the ship at Polyarnoe several Russian officers were entertained in the wardroom of *Obedient*, while down below the men indulged in that forces sing-song known to all as a 'Sod's Opera'. Paddy's suggestion that they go below and join in provoked a horrified response from the Russians – officers mixing socially with the lower ranks, whatever next!?

Convoy escort was a stressful affair with little time to relax, but there were occasional moments of humour. Commander Loftus Peyton-

Jones, DSC, DSO, RN, at the time a first lieutenant on board the destroyer *Achates*, related a story which may be apocryphal but may just as easily be true, concerning Richard Onslow, escort commander for *PQ16* in the destroyer *Ashanti*. The weather being fine, a *Luftwaffe* long-range reconnaissance seaplane had been circling the convoy just out of range of the escort's guns for hour after hour, relaying position, course and speed to waiting U-boats. This so irritated Commander Onslow that he is reputed to have signalled to the seaplane, 'You are making me dizzy – please go round the other way!' The German pilot must also have had a sense of humour, as he apparently complied with the request![11]

Progress up the slippery rope of promotion was no less sought after in war than in peacetime, and aboard the 17th Destroyer Flotilla leader HMS *Onslow*, Acting Leading Stoker Walter Watkin looked forward to confirmation of his rank. However, while the ship waited in Iceland to pick up convoy *JW51B*, Engineer Lieutenant Kevin Walton notified Watkin that the engineer commander had blocked his promotion for the time being as he had insufficient service time in the Royal Navy, and the appointment had gone to another rating. 'This did not go down very well with me as I had always been keen to do work on boilers, pumps, evaporator and distilling plant (changing sea water into pure distilled water) etc. However Kevin Walton told me there was no alternative.'[12] He may have been disappointed at missing his promotion at the time but, as events were to show, it was a disappointment which may have saved his life.

For the Germans service in the Arctic was also arduous, but with the considerable advantage that their ships operated from Norwegian ports, making long voyages in those storm-tossed latitudes less likely. Johann Hengel, EK11, U-Hunt & Mine Search Military Insignia, Destroyer-War Insignia, served as radio mate for 1½ years in the port protection flotilla based at Brest, and later as radio station commander in the torpedo boats *TA11* and *TA24* in the Mediterranean. Between these postings, he served as radio mate and guard commander in the main radio room of the destroyer *Z30* at the time of the Barents Sea action. In the summer of 1942 the twenty-one-year old was despatched with his kit bag and gun as his only companions, on the ore train from Germany through Denmark and Sweden to Narvik on the Norwegian coast. He recalled his arrival on board the destroyer, and service in the northern latitudes:

For me as a young mate reporting onboard *Z30* was a totally new experience. I was used to small boats, and this was a destroyer with a 300 man crew and a displacement of 3000 tons . . . At the beginning I found it very difficult to adjust to my new life because I was still a 'greenhorn'. This was also the way my new comrades treated me. But with an ability to assert myself I managed to become accepted. I had the advantage that I suffered less with seasickness than most of the others . . . Thanks to the seasickness of my comrades I happily received double meal allocations . . .[13]

Radio communications aboard *Z30* were carried out from two stations, the main radio room under the bridge and a second room aft which was manned during alerts. Johann Hengel's task during alerts was to man the aft station with two radio operators. He was also trained to be radio mate for a prize crew should a freighter be captured. *Z30* operated with the 5th Flotilla (North Sea), which later became the 8th Flotilla (Baltic Sea). Usually there would be six ships (half a flotilla) on station with the remainder at German yards for repairs and maintenance. The flotilla would often be based at Altenfjord, in company with *Tirpitz* and the mother ship controlling the *Luftwaffe* BV 138 reconnaissance aircraft scouring the Barents Sea for Allied shipping.

Despite the spectacular displays of the northern lights, long periods of almost perpetual darkness during the Arctic winter could be depressing for the German sailors (unlike their Allied opposite numbers, who welcomed the extra protection offered by the dark); however aboard *Z30*, even during these periods, if there were no operations planned there was usually something to do, as the ship had thirty pairs of skis onboard. Despite the inhospitable climate and the inevitable stresses and dangers of war, not all Johann Hengel's memories of Arctic service are bad:

The summer was a wonderful time, sunshine day and night . . . We tried to forget about the war, which we all hated . . . but nevertheless we did our duty. On occasion our destroyer berthed at the skerry of waterfalls, which enabled us ordinary seamen to take an extensive shower . . . We also sometimes went on shore leave into the mountains. Unexpectedly we found redcurrants, [and] in the early autumn we collected masses of mushrooms and blueberries on a lot of the islands. We would set out on small ships' boats to catch plaice with sticks.

One only likes to think back to life's good times.[14]

1 PRO. ADM 199/1104
2 Lt-Cdr Donovan, in conversation with the author
3 Ibid.
4 Ibid.
5 Captain Hutton, in correspondence with the author
6 Commander Loftus Peyton-Jones, in correspondence with the author
7 Lt-Cdr Albert Twiddy, in correspondence with the author
8 Lt-Cdr Donovan, in conversation with the author
9 Lt-Cdr Twiddy, in correspondence with the author
10 Ibid.
11 Cdr Peyton-Jones in correspondence with the author
12 Leading Stoker Walter Watkin, in correspondence with the author
13 Johann Hengel, in correspondence with the author
14 Ibid.

CHAPTER 3

THE BEST LAID PLANS . . .

Having accepted C-in-C Home Fleet Admiral Tovey's recommendation to run the December 1942 convoy through to Murmansk in two fifteen-ship sections, designated *JW51A* and *JW51B*, the Admiralty put in hand plans to assemble the necessary merchant ships, cargoes, and escorts. This last proved to be an extremely knotty problem (see p. 17). Stretched between operations in the Mediterranean, home waters, and the Atlantic, and unable to obtain destroyers from the United States due to the requirements of Operation *Torch*, it was decided to reduce the close escort from fifteen to seven destroyers, with a detached covering force of two light cruisers in the Barents Sea, plus the Home Fleet heavy ships operating to the westward. Anxious to avoid repeating the fate of the cruiser HMS *Edinburgh*, torpedoed and sunk by *U456* while part of the *QP11* escort, Admiral Tovey proposed that the cruisers should proceed no farther than 25°E, roughly the meridian of the North Cape (see map A, p. 144), in order to avoid the U-boats which gathered around the convoys from that point onwards. In this he was overruled by the First Sea Lord, who maintained that they should shadow the convoy all the way through to Murmansk. As Admiral Tovey was later freely to admit, it was extremely fortunate that they did so.

At *Kriegsmarine* Headquarters Northern Norway (*Gruppe Nord*), there had for some time been in existence a plan to attack Allied convoys using capital ships in a two-pronged pincer movement. Authorised by Grand Admiral Raeder to prepare for an operation against the next suitable target, Vice-Admiral Oskar Kummetz, *Befehlshaber der Kreuzer* (Admiral Commanding Cruisers -- BdK), opted to amend this plan for his attack, designated Operation *Regenbogen* (Rainbow). Assembling a powerful battle group comprising the heavy cruiser *Admiral Hipper* (flagship), pocket battleship *Lützow* and six destroyers, he would commence an offensive sweep from astern of the convoy – by attacking from west to east he would have the benefit of what little light was available, silhouetting the convoy against the eastern horizon. Kummetz calculated that at that time of year he would have two to three hours of twilight, approximately 9 a.m. to 12 noon, during which to make his attack. After that, his heavy ships would be particularly vulnerable to night torpedo attack from enemy destroyers, and he had at all times to keep in mind Hitler's strictures concerning minimum risk.

On locating the target he would take *Admiral Hipper*, (the faster of

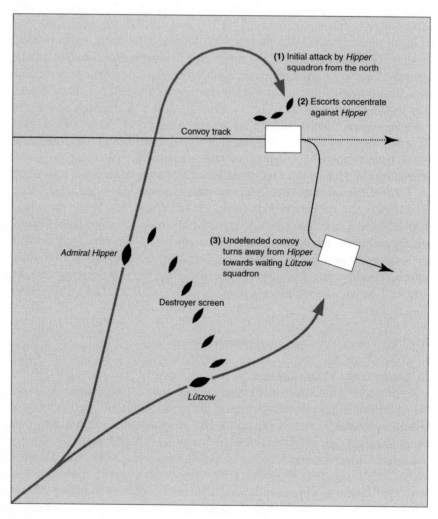

Operation *Regenbogen* – Admiral Kummetz's plan of attack (*Rodney L. Start, MBE, reproduced with the kind permission of Mrs Moira Start*)

the two heavy ships) with three destroyers to make an initial attack from the northward. He could then reasonably expect the defending destroyers to concentrate against his squadron, while the now undefended convoy turned south, away from *Hipper*'s attack – to be decimated by the waiting *Lützow* and her destroyers (see map, p. 32). As with any battle plan there were problems to be considered. The attack would be made in the depths of the Arctic winter, in what would almost certainly be adverse weather conditions with very little daylight; communications would inevitably be haphazard, and the attacking force would be split into two squadrons operating 75–85 miles (138–156 km) apart. Exceptional navigating skills and not a little luck would be required for the two attacking squadrons to arrive at their respective positions at the right time.

The Royal Navy 'O' class destroyers *Onslow, Obedient,* (Lt-Cdr D.C. Kinloch, RN), *Obdurate,* (Lt-Cdr C.E.L. Sclater, DSC, RN), *Oribi* and *Orwell* (Lt-Cdr N.H.G. Austen, DSO, RN) operated in the Arctic from the start of the Russia convoys, and by December 1942 were old hands at the tricky and dangerous business of 'riding shotgun' for the lumbering merchant ships. However Captain Robert St Vincent Sherbrooke, DSO, RN, had been in command of *Onslow* and Captain (D) (senior officer) of the flotilla for a matter of weeks only. The close escort for the second section of the December convoy, *JW51B,* would be his first Arctic command. In addition to the five 'O's Sherbrooke would have at his disposal two destroyers from the Clyde Special Escort Force (a small reserve force of destroyers, based at Gourock, to strengthen convoy escorts when necessary), *Achates* (Lt-Cdr A.H.T. Johns, RN) and *Bulldog* plus the corvettes *Hyderabad,* RIN, (Lt S.C.B. Hickman, RNR) and *Rhododendron* (Lt-Cdr L.A. Sayers, RN), minesweeper *Bramble* (Cdr H.T. Rust, DSO, RN) and the trawlers *Northern Gem* (Lt H.C. Aisthorpe, RNR) and *Vizalma* which, in the absence of rescue ships, would assist with rescue work. The seven destroyers would come under the collective umbrella of the 17th Destroyer Flotilla.

Captain Sherbrooke's instructions to the escort and merchant ships in the event of a surface attack were clear and concise. On sighting the enemy, five destroyers led by *Onslow* were to make a concerted attack, while the two remaining destroyers and all other escorts were to place themselves in the best position to make smoke between the convoy and the enemy. The merchantmen would turn by signal to the reciprocal of the bearing of the enemy (away from the attack),[1] the rear echelons and any other ships which could manage it laying smoke floats to cover their departure. As they were used to working together as a unit, the five 'O' class destroyers would form the attack force, while the remaining two would assist the other units of the close escort in laying smoke. Crucially, and in some measure due to serious fuel shortages, the five-destroyer group would confine itself to turning the enemy away by feinting torpedo attacks, and, having turned the attackers away would fall back on the convoy. Given the limited number of torpedoes available, only if a particularly favourable opportunity presented itself would they actually be launched. With their torpedoes gone, the destroyers would be virtually helpless against an attack by German heavy ships. Nevertheless, due to the caution normally displayed by commanders of the big German warships when faced by torpedo attack, it was anticipated that this tactic would have good prospects of success.

Captain Sherbrooke could obviously have had no knowledge of Vice-Admiral Kummetz's plan, but it can be seen that the convoy defence does in some measure fall in with Kummetz's expectations, with the vital exception that Sherbrooke rightly appreciated that the merchantmen were his principal concern, and had determined that the escort was not to be drawn too far from the convoy. The stage was therefore set for a lethal game of cat and mouse in the Arctic wastes.

Under the command of Rear-Admiral Robert Burnett a detached covering force, designated Force 'R', comprising as flagship the light cruiser *Sheffield* (Capt. Arthur Wellesley Clarke, RN), plus the light cruiser *Jamaica* (Capt. Jocelyn Latham Storey, RN), and one or two destroyers if available, would shadow both *JW51A* and *JW51B* through the Barents Sea at some 50 or so miles (92 km), distance.[2] A force of heavy ships from the Home Fleet would also be at sea some 300–400 miles (552–742 km) to the west, with the usual standing orders not to proceed east of Bear Island unless good prospects for catching German surface raiders at sea materialised. Cover was also to be provided for homeward-bound convoy *RA51*, due to sail from Murmansk around 30 December. This would principally comprise the destroyers which brought out *JW51A* as they became available.

Captain A.V. Radcliffe, RNR, Naval Control Service Officer at Loch Ewe, was not a happy man. Despite Admiralty assurances to the contrary, merchant ships were arriving at the loch unready for convoy service, placing a great strain on the limited resources available; and *JW51B* was no exception – the fifteen ships for this half of the convoy – British flag freighters *Empire Archer*, (the commodore's ship, Capt. R.A. Melhuish, RIN), *Daldorch*, *Dover Hill*, Panamanian flagged (US owned) *Ballot* and *Calobre*, US flagged *Chester Valley*, *Executive*, *Jefferson Myers*, *John H.B. Latrobe*, *Puerto Rican*, *Ralph Waldo Emerson*, *Vermont*, *Yorkmar*, and British flagged tankers *Empire Emerald* and *Pontfield* – all, with the exception of *Puerto Rican* and *Pontfield*, required some form of servicing. *Executive*, for example, had deck cargo damage, and required vegetables and 65 tons of water; *Ralph Waldo Emerson* required 150 tons of water and repairs to compasses and echo sounder, while the unhappy *Dover Hill* had both crew and engine troubles. In time-honoured tradition Captain Radcliffe arranged stores, sorted problems, and had the merchantmen ready to sail by the appointed day. He then settled down to compile another polite but frosty memo to the Director of Trade Division at the Admiralty.[3]

JW51A sailed from Loch Ewe on 15 December with a close escort of similar composition to *JW51B* and Force 'R', including the destroyers *Opportune* and *Matchless*, in attendance at the required distance. The convoy had fine weather, passed south of Bear Island and arrived off the Kola Inlet on Christmas Day, unmolested and in fact undiscovered by German forces. Force 'R' arrived at Vaenga in the Kola Inlet one day ahead of the convoy to refuel[4] and make ready to depart at short notice to cover *JW51B*.

With its precious cargo of 2046 vehicles, 202 tanks, 87 crated fighter aircraft, 33 crated bombers, 11,500 tons (11,684 tonnes) of fuel oil, 12,650 tons (12,852 tonnes) of aviation spirit, and 54,321 tons (55,190 tonnes) of general cargo (foodstuffs etc.),* *JW51B* slipped out of Loch Ewe late on 21 December into a crisp, clear night. Under the protective wing of Western Escort Group destroyers *Blankney*, *Chiddingfold*, *Ledbury*, and the minesweeper *Circe*, course was set for Seidisfjord on the eastern coast of Iceland, and the convoy was joined *en route* by elements of the close escort which would take it through to Murmansk – the corvettes *Hyderabad* and *Rhododendron*, the minesweeper *Bramble*

---

* These cargo values are an approximation, but are believed to be reasonably accurate.

and the trawlers *Vizalma* and *Northern Gem*. The 17th Destroyer Flotilla would join at Seidisfjord, where the Western Escort ships would depart.

22 December saw *JW51B* at sea, the five 'O' class destroyers fuelling at Seidisfjord, and *Achates*, in company with *Bulldog*,[5] *en route* to Iceland. It was now that the good weather, and good luck, which had accompanied *JW51A* began to desert *JW51B*. The two Clyde Special Escort Force destroyers, maintaining a good 16 knots in order to arrive by the 23rd, were hit by a southerly gale, force 12 (wind velocity in excess of 60 knots), forcing *Achates* to heave to (slow right down and lie in the most comfortable and safe position), to ride out the storm. *Bulldog* also lay hove-to for several hours, but she had a new commanding officer – new to the ship and new to the Arctic – who, believing that the storm was abating, announced his intention to proceed. On *Bulldog*'s bridge, navigating officer Eric Rhead, together with the first lieutenant, advised against attempting to continue in the existing conditions, particularly as the course to Seidisfjord lay across a very fierce sea. The commanding officer was adamant, however, and gave orders for the change of course and increased speed. Eric Rhead described the consequences:

> The inevitable happened and *Bulldog* charged into the gale . . . Most small ships have a breakwater on the forecastle as they normally ship a lot of water in bad weather at speed, and the breakwater just guides the water sideways back into the ocean. In our case the sea was too big, the speed to fast, with the result that the breakwater was just swept back, taking some five feet [1.52 m] of the forecastle deck with it, rather like opening a sardine tin. The crews quarters were swamped and indeed the ship was unsafe . . .[6]

As a result of this incident *Bulldog* was forced to return to the UK, and the small destroyer escort for *JW51B* was down to six.

JW51B found itself caught up in the same storm, which proved to be the last straw for *Dover Hill*, and she turned for home with weather damage and boiler trouble. The gale more or less blew itself out by the 24th and the weather cleared sufficiently for the *Luftwaffe* to launch reconnaissance missions that day. It is probable that this was the first inkling the Germans had of the convoy's existence, as a patrolling Focke-Wulf 200 Condor long-range maritime reconnaissance aircraft may well have spotted the ships at around 13.15 passing to the south of Iceland. Despite the unceasing efforts of her engine room personnel, *Empire Archer* proved to be an exceptionally bad 'smoker', which may have assisted the reconnaissance aircraft, and later *U354*, to home onto the convoy.

Achates arrived at Seidisfjord at 11.30 on the 24th with a catalogue of thankfully minor storm damages, and berthed alongside an oiler to top up with fuel. At 23.00 the same day the six ships of the 17th Destroyer Flotilla weighed anchor and followed *Onslow* out of the fjord to join *JW51B*. With the storm now past, weaving strands of aurora borealis flickered across the clear sky and as Christmas Day dawned, the destroyers formed up in line abreast and set course to rendezvous with the convoy some 150 miles (276 km) to the east.[7]

At 13.30 on Christmas Day the convoy was sighted, spread out in four columns and steering 320°. The 17th Destroyer Flotilla ships hurried stragglers into line, then took up their positions in the defensive screen, assisted by the Western Escort Group until nightfall when they were detached to Seidisfjord. By noon on the 26th the convoy was at 68°23' N 6°32' W, heading northward and crossing into the Arctic Circle at a steady 8½ knots. At these speeds destroyers encountered problems maintaining adequate steerage way, so would hold a speed some 2–3 knots faster but zigzag to an agreed pattern to maintain station with the merchantmen (and hopefully disrupt sightings by shadowing U-boats).

Noon on the 27th saw the convoy at 70°48' N, 00°22' W, making 8 knots. The weather was calm but bitterly cold, and as the ships pressed further north into the Arctic the hours of daylight became less and less. Also on the 27th Force 'R' sailed from the Kola Inlet going as far west as 11° E by the 29th and overlapping the patrol line of the Home Fleet battle group (battleship *Anson* and heavy cruiser *Cumberland*, plus destroyers) which, this being the limit of their patrol area, had turned back at 04.00 that same day. Force 'R' arrived some hours later (see map A, p. 144), despatching the two destroyers homeward while *Sheffield* and *Jamaica* turned east once again, Admiral Burnett setting a course well to the south of the convoy route.[8] The departure of Force 'R' from Kola was picked up by German intelligence and the information passed to Vice-Admiral Kummetz, but once out into the Barents Sea the British ships were missed by reconnaissance patrols, and Kummetz believed that they might be positioning themselves to escort homeward-bound convoy *RA51* which was then preparing to leave the inlet.

By noon on the 28th *JW51B* was in position 72°35' N, 4°20' E, course 071°. During the night the wind had increased to force 7 from the north-west, icing up was becoming a problem and heavy rolling seas had reduced the convoy's speed to 6½ knots. During the following night, the 28th/29th, the convoy was again struck by gale-force winds, now from north-north-west, and the ships experienced very heavy rolling. Several of the merchantmen encountered problems and *Jefferson Myers* was forced to heave to when her deck cargo came adrift (although Commodore Melhuish later stated that in his opinion to heave to and thus fall out of line was unnecessary, the problem, if anything, being inadequate stowage of deck cargo)[9]. It was a problem which would recur, and as the gale continued into the morning of the 29th deck cargo also broke loose on *Daldorch*. Between 01.00 and 12.00 that morning visibility swung from three cables (600 yd/548 m), to 1½ miles (2.77 km). The noon position was 73°19' N, 11°45' E, and by that afternoon the gale had at last begun to abate and visibility had increased to 10 miles (18 km). Only nine merchant ships could be seen in company, in ragged order, and the trawler *Vizalma* and destroyer *Oribi* had also become detached from the main body during the night. As the weather continued to improve, *Bramble*, which had better radar equipment than most of the escort, was sent in search of stragglers and the speed of the convoy reduced to 6 knots to enable them to catch up. At 23.59 on the 29th course was altered to 090°, due east.

1   PRO. ADM 199/73
2   PRO. ADM 234/369. Admiral Tovey, still concerned at the U-boat threat, laid down instructions that the cruisers were not to close within 50 miles (92 km) of the convoys unless enemy surface craft were located.
3   PRO. ADM 199/73
4   PRO. ADM 234/369
5   While part of the escort for Atlantic convoy *OB318* in May 1941, *Bulldog* attacked, forced to the surface and captured, *U110*. On board the U-boat an *Enigma* machine was discovered with signal set, along with many confidential books and papers. This was the first of the prized German coding machines to be captured and was sent to Bletchley Park where it greatly assisted British code-breakers to crack the German naval codes. See Smith, Michael (2000) *Station X*, Channel 4 Books.
6   Rhead, Cdr Eric Bertrand, DSC, *Paddling My Own Canoe: The Autobiography of a Sailor*, unpublished. Quoted with kind permission of Mrs Helen Rhead.
7   Memoir (unpublished) of Commander Loftus Peyton-Jones, supplied to the author. As a first lieutenant, Commander Peyton-Jones served aboard HMS *Achates* at the time, and subsequent descriptions of events concerning this ship are largely based on his recollections.
8   PRO. ADM 234/369
9   PRO. ADM 199/73. Commodore's report.

British flagged SS *Daldorch*, to which the convoy vice-commodore transferred after *Calobre* sustained splinter damage while under fire from *Lützow* (*Photo: World Ship Society Photograph Library*)

SS *Jefferson Myers*, one of several US flagged merchant vessels with convoy *JW51B* (*Photo: World Ship Society Photograph Library*)

Matilda tanks on the quayside at a British port, waiting to be loaded aboard merchant ships bound for Russia (*Photo: IWM H 14786*)

Two Russian front-line nurses, Anya Vesnicheva and Antonia Dogina, enjoy chocolate sent from Britain. Nurse Anya, left, displays the medal awarded to her for exceptional bravery in the face of the enemy (*Photo: IWM RUS 4293*)

2nd Lt J.P. 'Paddy' Donovan, shore leave, summer 1942
(*Photo: Lt-Cdr J.P. Donovan*)

Paddy Donovan in full Arctic kit aboard HMS *Obedient*, winter 1942/3 (*Photo: Lt-Cdr J.P. Donovan*)

41

The crew of 'A' turret, HMS *Sheffield* – Midshipman Twiddy standing fourth from right *(Photo: IWM A19971)*

Chipping ice from chains, wires, and bollards on the forecastle. Temperatures could plunge to –50 degrees Celsius, and the extreme frost would 'weld' ungloved hands to metal. (*Photo: IWM A 6856*)

'There were no *ENSA* comedians or dancing girls in North Russia.' Members of *Sheffield*'s crew put on some homegrown entertainment (*Photo: Lt-Cdr A.W. Twiddy*)

Leading Stoker Walter Watkin, pictured
on leave from HMS *Onslow*
(*Photo: Ldg Stoker Walter Watkin*)

Midshipman Albert Twiddy (left),
shortly before joining HMS *Sheffield*,
1942 (*Photo: Lt-Cdr A.W. Twiddy*)

The German pocket battleship *Lützow*, a formidable opponent for the convoy destroyer escort (*Photo: IWM HU1049*)

The German Narvik class destroyer *Z30*. Note single 5.9 in (146 mm) turret forward, instead of the excessively heavy twin turret with which a number of the class were fitted. *(Photo: W.Z. Bilddienst)*

Lieutenant-Commander Heinrich Kaiser, the longest-serving commander of *Z30* (*Photo: Johann Hengel*)

'High up north, 13 November 1942.' A cosy grog evening in the 'U-room', *Z30.* Johann Hengel far left (*Photo: Johann Hengel*)

Ships of the German 5th (later 8th) Destroyer Flotilla against the spectacular backdrop of Narvikfjord

Johann Hengel, right, on leave,
February 1943 (*Photo: Johann Hengel*)

CHAPTER 4

FOG OF WAR

Kapitänleutnant Karl-Heinz Herschelb and *U354* shadowed *JW51B* from the morning of 30 December, and shortly after noon reported the convoy to Admiral Commanding Northern Waters Otto Kluber at Narvik, as '6–10 steamers Qu 6394 AB, enemy on course 100°. Poorly secured convoy protected by several destroyers up to one light cruiser.'[1]

Later that afternoon Herschelb tried a torpedo attack, reporting: 'Convoy in square AC 4189, widely spaced, large zigzags on a mean course of 080 degrees, about 10 steamships, several destroyers, 1 cruiser doubtful. Spread salvo of three missed on account of zig-zagging. Weather is good apart from short snow squalls.'[2]

Covered by dark *U354* surfaced on the starboard quarter of the convoy, tracking the merchant ships through hydrophones by the slow rhythmic churning of their propellers until another echo materialised, its source rapidly closing. This could only mean a destroyer approaching at high speed, and *U354* slipped quickly beneath the waves.

By 00.45 on the 30th word had come through to Captain Sherbrooke that *Vizalma* and the freighter *Chester Valley* were together, but some distance to the north of the main body of the convoy, which was itself 13 miles (24 km), south of its anticipated position thanks to the gale of the previous night. At 11.30 ships were sighted on bearing 200° 9 miles (16.7 km) distant and *Obdurate* was sent to investigate, returning by 14.00 with two of the missing freighters. The noon position was 73°27' N, 19°35' E, and speed was reduced to 8 knots to allow the missing ships to catch up. At 20.20 the alarm was sounded as *Obdurate* sped to investigate a possible submarine on the surface. She was joined by *Obedient* and both hunted the elusive echo and dropped depth charges, but were not convinced that it had been a submarine after all. They were also unable to contact *Hyderabad*, which should have been in a good position to join the hunt.[3] This would be the first of a number of communications problems with the corvette over the ensuing twenty-four hours. Most worrying for Sherbrooke, *Oribi* had still not rejoined. She had in fact been struggling with a defective gyrocompass and after trying vainly to find the convoy proceeded on to Murmansk. She would be badly missed; the destroyer escort was now down to five.

Rear-Admiral Burnett, with Force 'R', proposed, for reasons similar to those expressed by Vice-Admiral Kummetz, to cross the convoy's wake, take position to the north and shadow from some 40–50 miles (75–92 km) astern so that he would have the advantage of any available light[4] should an attack develop. Additionally, in that position his cruisers would be less likely to attract the attention of any air reconnaissance which might then be drawn on to the convoy. He had several problems to contend with in arriving at his intended covering position by 31 December, however. Rear-Admiral Burnett considered this to be the crucial time given the expected position of the convoy at that point, and the fact that any attacking German surface ships would almost certainly sortie from Altenfjord (see map, p. 52).

Since leaving the Kola Inlet the weather had been so overcast that it had not been possible to take sightings from the stars, obliging navigating officers to calculate their position using 'dead reckoning'. To complicate matters further Rear-Admiral Burnett had no sightings of the convoy, the only report he had of its position being a message received from C-in-C Home Fleet, Admiral Tovey, timed at 11.21 on 27 December. This estimated that *JW51B* would pass the longitude of Bear Island at 16.00 on the 29th, whereas in fact this point was passed at around 12.00 the following day, the convoy being some 150 miles (276 km) further west, and as already noted, some way south of its intended position (see map, p. 52).[5] Having no option but to assume that C-in-C Home Fleet's message was accurate, at 18.00 on the 30th Rear-Admiral Burnett gave orders for Force 'R' to come around to course 320° and proceed so as to be in a covering position to the north and astern of the convoy by dawn. In fact, as can be seen from the map, the cruisers passed ahead of the convoy and by 08.30 on the 31st were some 30 miles (55 km) due north of the merchantmen.

Admiral Kluber in Narvik passed *U354*'s sightings to Vice-Admiral Kummetz on 30 December, and ordered him to bring his battle group to three-hour stand-by. Consequently early that afternoon Kummetz summoned his captains aboard *Admiral Hipper* to outline his plan of attack; those present represented *Hipper* (*Kapitän zur See* Hans

Hartmann), *Lützow*, (*Kapitän zur See* Rudolf Stange) and the destroyers *Friedrich Eckholdt* (Capt. Alfred Schemmel, Commander 5th Destroyer Flotilla, doubling as captain of *Eckholdt* as her own captain, Lt-Cdr Lutz Gerstung, had died a few days earlier), *Richard Beitzen* (Lt-Cdr Hans von Davidson), *Theodor Riedel* (Lt-Cdr Walter Riede), *Z29* (Lt-Cdr Curt Rechel), *Z30* (Lt-Cdr Heinrich Kaiser) and *Z31* (Lt-Cdr Hermann Alberts).

Having ensured that his senior officers fully understood his strategy, Vice-Admiral Kummetz closed the meeting with a summary of his intended battle tactics:

> At night I cannot attack the convoy . . . for on principle our own ships should not be exposed to nocturnal attack from destroyers . . . The only thing left is to make use of the few hours of polar twilight that in these latitudes count for daylight . . . By dawn we should have closed the

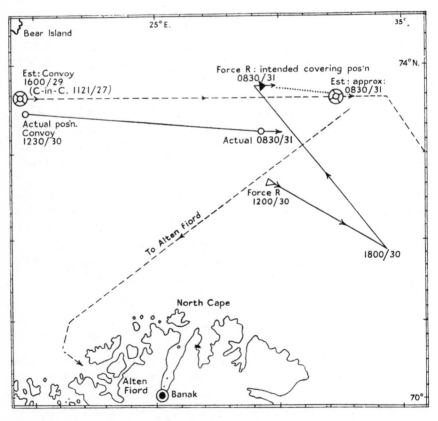

Force 'R' 12.00 hrs, 30 December to 08.30 hrs 31 December *(PRO. ADM. 234/369)*

enemy. The main objective then is first the destruction of the security force, and after that the merchantmen, with special emphasis on immobilising as many as possible by gunfire in the shortest possible time . . .[6]

At 14.10 that afternoon Kummetz received a radio message from Narvik requesting the time of departure of the battle group and giving the estimated position of '*PQ20*' (German intelligence had not yet picked up the prefix switch from *PQ* to *JW*), the following day. Paragraph 4 of this message reads:

A. Bringing in of single steamers very desirable.
B. No loss of time due to rescuing . . . enemy crews.
C. Only some prisoner captains and crew for interrogation of value.
D. Rescue of enemy crews by enemy forces not desirable.[7]

Neither Allied or Axis ships would stop for rescue missions, of friend or foe, if it was thought that by so doing they would put themselves in danger; however an order not to rescue enemy crews under any circumstances highlights the low value placed on human life by the Nazi High Command, ultimately that of their own population as well as those of their enemies.

By 30 December *U626* (*Oberleutnant* Hans-Helmuth Bugs) had also made contact with *JW51B* and good intelligence as to the convoy's movements was therefore anticipated. In fact at this time Kummetz almost certainly had a better idea of the convoy's location than Rear-Admiral Burnett; however to compensate for this to some degree Burnett's cruisers had still not been located, the balance of probability for the German command being that they were homeward-bound with convoy *RA51*.

With the German battle group making preparations for sea, down the chain of command came the first note of caution, contained in a radio message from Narvik: 'Conduct towards the enemy: Avoid superior enemy, otherwise destroy if in [advantageous] tactical situation.'[8]

The German chain of command for most naval operations was cumbersome in the extreme, and for *Regenbogen* comprised the following, who were all directly involved:

Adolf Hitler at Wolfschanze to:
the *Kriegsmarine* representative at *Führer* Headquarters Admiral Theodore Krancke to:

Grand Admiral Raeder, Berlin, to:
Admiral Rolf Carls, C-in-C *Gruppe Nord*, Kiel, to:
Admiral Otto Kluber, Admiral Commanding Northern Waters, Narvik to:
Vice-Admiral Oskar Kummetz at Altenfjord.

With the estimated time of departure for the battle group initially set at 17.00, *Admiral Hipper*'s perennial engine problems (see Appendix I), struck again when a flange on the starboard condenser pump was found to be blowing, risking failure of the starboard engine should it worsen. Following an inspection Kummetz decided that repairs would be possible while at sea (their estimated duration was twelve hours), and a departure time of 18.00 was fixed.

At 16.37 *U354* had reported to Narvik: 'Convoy Qu. 4189 AC has spread out, large jags [zigzags] around 80°, approximately 10 steamers, several destroyers, 1 cruiser doubtful . . . Weather good except for short squalls of snow.'[9]

This information was passed to Vice-Admiral Kummetz, followed at 16.48 by another exhortation to exercise caution from Admiral Kluber: 'Commander: Contrary to op.-command [see message above] conduct towards the enemy: Exercise restraint even when enemy is equally matched as cruisers should not take big risks.'[10]

If the German high command had deliberately set out to hamstring Vice-Admiral Kummetz they could not have done a better job – and they were not finished yet! The battle group departed Altenfjord via Lopphavet Sound and set course to clear the coast, and British submarine patrols,[11] at 24 knots, the maximum speed of *Lützow*. A short time into the voyage mechanical problems struck again as destroyer *Z31* developed a fault with her port engine, and speed was reduced to 18 knots to enable her to maintain contact. By 22.55 the battle group had reached position 71°01' N, 21°25' E, and course was altered to 060° to intercept the convoy. Shortly thereafter *Z31* reported her engine problem solved, and speed increased to 24 knots.

By 02.00 on New Year's Eve dead reckoning placed the German battle group at 71°36' N, 24°38' E, at which point Kummetz deployed his attack formation (see diagram p. 32). His reconnaissance screen of six destroyers was to sweep eastwards 15 miles (28 km) apart, with *Hipper* 15 miles astern the northern wing destroyer, and *Lützow* 15 miles astern the southern wing destroyer. *Lützow* had orders to be 75 miles (138 km) and 180° from *Hipper* at 08.00, by which time the flagship would be at position 73°40' N, 28° E.

The vice-admiral's appreciation of the position at this point was as follows:

> 1. I consider the most recent location report of the submarine in contact at 16.37 to be reliable, as it can easily be connected to the previous location reports. I therefore take it as a starting point for the approach to the reconnaissance formation.

> 2. The escort convoy is fast but moves jaggedly, so I assume general course to be no faster than approx. 8 nm [knots]. If the enemy goes in a straight line for a longer period of time, their advancing speed will increase accordingly. I reckon the enemy is trying to gain space to the east. I also have to take a slow rotation into a southern direction into account. I think, though, that due to his respect for the German air force he will not get too close to the coastline. He will try to shake off the covering submarines by going jaggedly, supported by the weather conditions, which are unfavourable for submarines.

> 3. The reconnaissance formation has to cover the most probable voyage speeds of between 7 and approximately 11 nm, and the most probable courses between 85 to approximately 110°.

> 4. I want to run into the escort convoy with . . . favourable lookout conditions and the enemy . . . visible against the light horizon as dawn breaks. I therefore put up with the unfavourable torpedo tactic situation.[12]

At 05.00 *Hipper* picked up a radio message dispatched by *U354* to Narvik which read, 'From 20.30 forced under water, bombed. Last location escort Qu. 4513 AC, [course] around 120° 13 nm, weather conditions very good, advancing . . .'[13]

This showed a more southerly course for the convoy than anticipated, and although he was sceptical of its accuracy, Kummetz could not afford to ignore it since if his target now held to 120° he would miss it completely if he made no adjustment. He therefore shifted the destroyer screen 20 miles (37 km) to the south. Being less sure of the enemy position, and despite the possibility that the transmissions might betray the battle group's location, Kummetz ordered that from 06.00 onwards, whenever visibility dropped below 6 miles (11.5 km), all ships should use FuMG radar every ten minutes for two minutes at a time in order to avoid running into the convoy unexpectedly.

Bearing in mind that this was *Kapitän zur See* Stange's first operational command, the higher echelons of German naval authority had prepared something of a surprise for him and *Lützow* at this late stage in the proceedings. At 05.45 he received the following from Admiral Kluber in Narvik (copied to *Hipper*):

> FT 01.53 from North Sea Commander SSD to B.d.K and *Lützow*:
> 1. After completion *Regenbogen* intending to release *Lützow* within the North Sea northwards 70 degrees north between 5 degrees east and 35 degrees east.
> 2. Mission: cruiser-war, detect enemy shipping traffic, attack single cruisers and poorly secured escorts. Cue for release *Aurora* . . .
> 3. Development of *Regenbogen* is crucial for release . . . Proceed only if *Lützow* has at least half of artillery and torpedo ammunition left.
> 4. Break off *Lützow*'s being at sea independently as soon as enemy units can be recognised from heavy cruiser upwards or after collection of enemy forces becomes probable following considerable success . . . Further information later.[14]

It is probably fair to say that Rudolf Stange was not the most resourceful captain in the *Kriegsmarine*, but it is not difficult to understand his consternation on receipt of this radio communication on the point of engaging the convoy, particularly as the message contains its fair share of 'ifs', 'buts', and 'maybes'. As Stange himself commented: 'The receipt of this FT creates a new situation for me in so far as contrary to the original plans . . . it is now no longer possible to talk the operation through with B.d.K in detail, neither can I request documents about the enemy from him . . .'[15]

Whether Vice-Admiral Kummetz knew that this operation within an operation was in the wind is open to question, but, crucially, it appears that Stange did not, which may go some way towards explaining his performance in the engagement which followed.

At 07.18 two shadows bearing 060° were sighted by *Admiral Hipper*, and *Friedrich Eckholdt* was sent to investigate. At 07.47 a large shadow was sighted and *Hipper* turned towards it on course 110°. This may have been one of the tankers straggling astern of the convoy, and may initially have been mistaken for a cruiser by the approaching German force. As Kummetz and *Kapitän zur See* Hartmann considered their options six more shadows were identified, and both officers were now certain that this must be the convoy. By 08.00 *Lützow* was in position and reporting a moderate swell, clouds and occasional snow showers. In *Kapitän zur See* Stange's estimation the convoy was some

80 miles (148 km) to the north, caught between the jaws of the German 'pincers' – which he now prepared to close.

Despite the apparent complexities of his plan Vice-Admiral Kummetz had placed his forces perfectly, and at 07.58 he signalled his sighting to the battle group: 'Alarm Square 4395.'[16]

As darkness struggled toward twilight that 31 December, *JW51B* consisted of twelve merchantmen (two stragglers still absent), accompanied by five destroyers, two corvettes and a trawler. The convoy's course was easterly, position approximately 220 miles (408 km) north-west of the Kola Inlet. Some 45 miles (82 km) to the north the trawler *Vizalma* with the freighter *Chester Valley* in company attempted to rejoin the main body, while some 15 miles (28 km) to the north-east the minesweeper *Bramble* still looked for stragglers. Rear-Admiral Burnett with Force 'R' was approximately 30 miles (55 km) north of the convoy and 15 miles south of *Vizalma*. None of these four groups had any idea of the positions of the others, and there was also another straggler somewhere in the area.[17]

The weather was for the most part clear, the twilight visibility being around 7 miles (13 km) to the north, 10 miles (18.5 km) to the south. At intervals however, visibility was much reduced by snow squalls. There was low cloud cover, wind west-north-west force 3, sea slight, 16 degrees of frost, and ice on all ships.[18]

At about 08.20 *Hyderabad*, astern the convoy on the starboard wing (see diagram, p. 58), sighted two unidentified ships crossing the convoy's wake. She had previously picked up a coded radio message notifying the convoy to expect two Russian aircraft, an incorrect decode unfortunately substituting 'destroyers' for 'aircraft'. The corvette took these to be the Russian ships, and did not pass the information on. At 08.30 *Obdurate*, on the convoy's starboard beam, reported to *Onslow*: 'Bearing 210 2 destroyers.'[19]

It was at first considered that these might be *Oribi* and *Bramble*, but *Obdurate* was sent to investigate. A sixth sense seems to have warned Captain Sherbrooke that this might be trouble, for as *Obdurate* commenced her sweep astern of the convoy he ordered *Onslow*'s complement sent to breakfast and to change into clean underwear – a naval tradition dating back to the days of the wooden wall sailing ships to help guard against infection in the event of wounding. A tense hour passed, until at 09.29 gun flashes were seen by *Onslow* in the direction taken by *Obdurate*. Sherbrooke ordered *Orwell* and *Obedient* to join him, the latter having to come around and astern of the convoy. The two destroyers spotted by *Obdurate* turned out to be three, and were in fact *Friedrich Eckholdt*, *Richard Beitzen* and *Z29*, the three destroyers which completed *Hipper*'s squadron, opening from *Lützow*'s group to the south. The three German destroyers turned to the north-west away from *Obdurate*, but when she closed to 8000 yds (7300 m), *Eckholdt* opened fire. The British destroyer turned away to rejoin the convoy, while the German trio continued on to the north-west to close on *Hipper*.

As *Onslow* and *Orwell* sped to investigate the gunfire and *Obedient* hurried to catch up, *Achates*, complying with Captain Sherbrooke's instructions, assisted the three smaller escorts to lay smoke covering the convoy.

Anticipating engaging an enemy destroyer force, at 09.39 *Onslow*'s

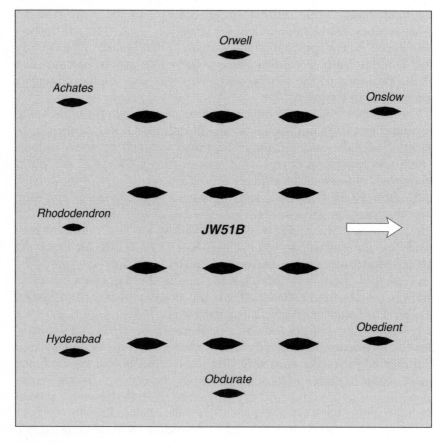

Escort dispositions, morning, 31 December 1942 (*Rodney L. Start, MBE, reproduced with the kind permission of Mrs Moira Start*)

58

first officer, Lieutenant-Commander Thomas Marchant, drew Sherbrooke's attention to an altogether more formidable opponent bearing 325° (fine on *Onslow*'s starboard bow), distance 8 miles (15 km), on a course of 140°. As this large warship turned to port to bring all her main armament to bear, Marchant recognised her as the *Admiral Hipper*, and at 09.41 the German cruiser opened fire on *Achates*, clearly visible to the south. Sherbrooke decided to attack with the two destroyers present and opened fire at an approximate range of 9000 yards (8229 m).

At this point the problems of fighting a ship in the Arctic became uncomfortably apparent, as only the flotilla leader's 'B' turret was firing; 'Y' turret was not yet bearing and 'A' and 'X' turrets were out of action due to a thin film of ice having formed in the recesses behind the extractor.[20] Fortunately for the British destroyers it was assumed by *Hipper* that they were making a torpedo attack, and she sheered away to port. The two escorts positioned themselves to keep between *Hipper* and the convoy.

The big German cruiser had been firing for a matter of minutes only, but she had been effective. Onboard *Achates* gun flashes could be seen to the north, and *Hipper*'s shells began to fall uncomfortably close, throwing up great fountains of water as they exploded on impact. Lieutenant-Commander Johns ordered speed increased, and *Achates* heeled over under the helm, zigzagging in an attempt to throw off the enemy's gunnery. Despite this the next salvo was closer, huge geysers of water erupting on either side of the ship. Two more salvos were equally close, one near-miss exploding on the port side abreast of the bridge of the speeding destroyer, drenching gun crews in icy spray and sending showers of splinters scything across the deck. As *Hipper* turned away she ceased firing, and *Achates'* crew was left to assess the damage.[21]

Sent to investigate, Lieutenant Loftus Peyton-Jones soon discovered that although no direct hits had been suffered, the damage was serious. Going below he found that numerous splinters from the big 8 in (203 mm) shells had cut through the thin plating of the destroyer's hull, creating havoc between the decks. Electric leads were cut, and lockers and mess tables, broken loose from their fastenings, were crashing from side to side as the ship rolled. In the dim light it was difficult not to trip over the killed and wounded who lay in the passageways and messdecks, but the ship's doctor, James MacFarlane, was already at work organising removal of the injured to first-aid posts, and quieting those more seriously hurt with shots of morphia.

On the forward messdeck repair parties attempted to plug the holes through which water spurted as the ship rolled to port, while on the stokers' messdeck below a stream of water entered through a fractured hull plate. During *Achates*'s last refit insulation had been fitted to the messdecks to make life more tolerable in Arctic waters, and this now had to be torn away to get to the hull plating. It proved to be a difficult and time-consuming job. Finally it was decided to close the forward magazine, shell room and stokers' messdeck, and shore up the bulkheads on either side. To ease the pressure on the damaged hull speed was reduced, but *Achates* continued with her principal task, and patrolled to and fro, covering the convoy with smoke.[22]

At 09.45,[23] as *Hipper* and the two British destroyers skirmished, the convoy turned from east to south-east and maintained a speed of 9 knots. By 09.55 *Obedient* had joined Sherbrooke and *Obdurate* could be seen returning from her brush with *Friedrich Eckholdt.* The enemy destroyers concerned Sherbrooke as they had not been sighted in the engagement with *Hipper,* and he believed they might be attempting to attack the merchantmen; consequently he ordered *Obedient* and *Obdurate* to rejoin the convoy to cover such an eventuality, although in fact Kummetz had ordered his three consorts to maintain station with the flagship. The action was barely fifteen minutes old, but Kummetz had been suitably impressed by the tactics of the British destroyers, stating in his report:

> The destroyers are . . . remarkably versatile. They push in between the convoy and *Hipper* in a way that it is not possible to get to the steamers. They are using a very effective artificial fog, trying to cover up the steamers. With evasive manoeuvres and by seeking shelter in the fog and smoke area they are cleverly trying to escape the artillery fire from *Hipper.* Their position to each other shows *Hipper* in danger from torpedoes, even when she moves towards them directly for a higher artillery effect and to use the artillery against the steamers.[24]

At 10.08 *Obedient* turned away to southward and signalled *Obdurate* to join her, the two laying smoke to screen the wake of the convoy before joining it. Sherbrooke's force was now stretched very thin, but at 09.55 he had received very good news indeed from *Sheffield* : 'Am approaching on course of 170°.[25]

By 08.45 that morning Force 'R', with Rear-Admiral Burnett still under the impression that he was positioning his cruisers astern of the convoy, remained on a north-westerly heading at 17 knots, approximate position 73° 47' N, 28° 54' E.[26] At 08.58 a radio direction finder (RDF) contact was obtained bearing 320° (dead ahead), at a range of 14,900 yards, (13,624 m). Some minutes later a ship could dimly be made out on this bearing, her course and speed estimated to be 090° at 25 knots. It was necessary for Rear-Admiral Burnett to establish the identity of the contact so he altered course away to the south-east, coming around to a north-easterly bearing to close on the mystery ship in order to track her further (see map B, p. 146). By this time the original speed calculation for the target had proved to be incorrect and was now estimated to be 10 knots.[27] At around 09.30 gun flashes were seen to the south as the German destroyers opened on *Obdurate*; however aboard *Sheffield* it was thought that this might be anti-aircraft fire, and in any event it quickly died away. Rear-Admiral Burnett was still not satisfied with the identity of the radar contact, and continued to track it for another quarter of an hour until heavy gunfire was observed to the south, and a report of three enemy destroyers was received from Captain Sherbrooke.

It now appeared to Rear-Admiral Burnett that the mysterious radar contact must in all probability be stragglers from the convoy[28] and at 09.55 he ordered Force 'R' around to the south on a course of 170°, and in line ahead *Sheffield* and *Jamaica* worked up to their maximum 32 knots.

In some respects it does seem that Force 'R' might have made for the gunfire sooner. The mystery echo, a potential enemy, had to be checked; however the best part of an hour had been taken up with this endeavour. The confused situation on the day must of course be taken into consideration, particularly keeping in mind that the prime consideration was the safe arrival of the convoy, allied to Rear-Admiral Burnett's belief that *JW51B* was 150 miles (277 km) or more east of the position from which the firing emanated.

As Force 'R' headed southwards *Admiral Hipper* continued skirmishing with the British destroyers, running in to engage them with her secondary and anti-aircraft guns, while firing over them at the convoy with her main armament. Partly as a result of caution concerning torpedo attack and partly to try to draw the destroyers away from the convoy, with the range down to around 11,000 yards (10,000 m), Kummetz would swing away to the north, subsequently repeating the manoeuvre. Between the twilight visibility, snow squalls, and smoke laid by the British destroyers, the 'fog of war' had begun to take on a literal definition so whether *Obedient* and *Obdurate* were observed from the German flagship returning to the convoy is not certain. Perhaps Vice-Admiral Kummetz was aware that the convoy had turned away toward the *Lützow* squadron and he wished to be in at the kill, but whatever his reasoning, shortly after 10.00 he seems to have determined that as they would not be drawn away from the merchantmen, he would concentrate on the troublesome destroyers, and instructed *Kapitän zur See* Hartmann to clear them from his path once and for all.[29]

1   Kummetz, Vice-Admiral *War Diary of Operation* Regenbogen, Bundesarchiv. Translated from the original German.
2   Ibid.
3   PRO. ADM 199/73
4   In latitude 73° N at this time of year, the sun at no time rises above 6° below the horizon (civil twilight). Nautical twilight (12° below horizon) starts at about 08.00 and ends about 14.50. In late December 1942 the moon (3rd quarter) set about 11.10. PRO. ADM 234/369
5   PRO. ADM 234/369
6   Bekker, Cajus (1974) *Hitler's Naval War*, Macdonald & Jane's.
7   Kummetz, op. cit.
8   Ibid.
9   Ibid.
10 Ibid.
11 There were four British submarines at that time off the northern coast of Norway: *Unruly, Trespasser, Seadog* and *Graph* – the former German *U570*, uniquely captured by one of Coastal Command's Hudson bombers in August 1941.
12 Kummetz, op. cit.
13 Ibid.
14 Stange, *Kapitan zur See*, Lützow *War Diary*, Bundesarchiv. Translated from the original German.
15 Ibid.
16 Kummetz, op. cit.
17 PRO. ADM 234/369
18 Ibid.
19 PRO. ADM 199/73
20 PRO. ADM 234/492
21 Memoir of Commander L.E. Peyton-Jones, supplied to the author.
22 Ibid.
23 According to *Obedient*'s report, although according to the Commodore's report (ADM 199/73), the convoy altered course at 10.20.
24 Kummetz, op. cit.
25 PRO. ADM 199/73
26 PRO. ADM 1/14217
27 PRO. ADM 234/369. The primitive nature of radar in 1942 should be kept in mind. In *Sheffield*, bearings and ranges would be passed by voice pipe, and the operators would be using new equipment with necessarily very little experience of using it on active duty.
28 It was in fact *Vizalma* and *Chester Valley*, who had altered course to the east having also seen the gunfire.
29 While Vice-Admiral Kummetz was in overall command, much of the actual fighting of the German flagship would have been handled by *Kapitän zur See* Hartmann (much the same relationship would have existed between Rear-Admiral Burnett and Captain Storey aboard *Sheffield*). Hartmann for one seems to have favoured a more aggressive approach than the one inflicted on them by the high command, Kummetz reporting that he had to 'hold him back' during the course of the battle.

CHAPTER 5

'THE WHOLE PLACE WAS ALIGHT'

Admiral Hipper's first couple of salvos fell well over *Onslow*, which returned fire, and at 10.14 observers on the destroyers saw a faint flash on the cruiser amidships.[1] *Hipper*'s next salvo passed 'uncomfortably close and over' *Onslow*[2] followed in quick succession by two 150 yards over, and two more straddling the stern. The cruiser now had the range and the next salvo fell either side of the destroyer's bridge, one shell exploding close to the port side, splinters peppering the torpedomen's messdeck. At 10.18 *Onslow* was again straddled, one shell striking the top of the funnel. Both RDF sets and all her main radio telephone aerials were destroyed, and a hail of splinters sprayed across the bridge. Lieutenant-Commander Marchant remembered that 'a splinter passed between me and Captain (D).'[3] The splinter hit Captain Sherbrooke in the face, badly wounding him and temporarily blinding his left eye. There was no let-up in the pounding as another salvo from *Hipper* immediately struck home with direct hits to the destroyer's superstructure under 'B' turret, and the forecastle abreast 'A' turret.[4] Fires were now taking hold in the fore part of the stricken destroyer and Sherbrooke, refusing to leave the bridge until his ship was out of danger, ordered her to make smoke and turn to starboard. The turn upset *Hipper*'s gunnery and the next three salvos fell harmlessly some 30 yards (27 m) away. However Kummetz must have believed that the enemy flotilla leader was finished, as he shifted his fire to *Orwell*.

As the shells struck *Onslow*, Acting Stoker Walter Watkin had been making his way forward with Engineer Lieutenant Kevin Walton, both intending to assist the fire and repair party stationed in the after seamen's messdeck located immediately below 'A' and 'B' turrets. Lieutenant Walton broke the glass front of a locker holding a fire hose and handed the hose to Watkin. A standpipe containing sea water under pressure was located close to the funnel, and Watkin dashed back to connect the hose. As he did so he saw the wounded chief stoker lying on the deck and sliding under the guardrail as the ship heeled over to starboard. Grabbing the injured man he dragged him inboard and propped him up by the funnel, then connecting the hose to the standpipe he opened the valve and dragged the hose back to fight the fires in the seamen's messdeck. He recalls that 'the whole place was alight, with fires burning fiercely. The steel structure was a mass of twisted metal, and dead bodies [were] lying around.'[5] As the two men played water on the fire it must have been apparent to Watkin that the entire fire and repair party had been wiped out when their repair station received a direct hit. It might also have occurred to him, as it certainly did later when he had time to reflect, that had he received the promotion he had wanted, he would have been a member of that party.

One fire in particular was proving difficult to get at. Handing the hose to another rating, Lieutenant Walton and Walter Watkin made their way to the main deck forward, where Walton believed he could get at the fire by going down through the shell hole in the forecastle. Dense smoke billowed from the hole and he had no way of knowing whether the deck below had been shot away. Nevertheless, with a handkerchief tied over his nose and mouth he lashed a rope around his chest and handed it to Watkin, who lowered him down. He had two hoses fed down to him and fought the fires there for twenty minutes before being relieved.

With Walton out of the forecastle, Watkin heard a shout that fires had spread to the engine room artificers' (ERAs') messdeck beneath the captain's sea cabin and the bridge. Going back to the area he arranged for a bucket party to fill buckets from a lavatory and pass them to him as he stood at the top of a ladder and threw water over the bulkhead of the ERAs' pantry, which blistered with heat from the fire on the other side. An ERA arrived with a fire hose, and opening the door to the messdeck played water on the red-hot bulkheads. Watkin was subsequently instructed to go below and take over watch-keeping duties in No.1 boiler room.[6]

Having received damage reports and ensured that *Onslow* was out of immediate danger, Captain Sherbrooke transferred command of the 17th Destroyer Flotilla to Commander Kinloch of *Obedient*, remaining on the bridge until an acknowledgement was obtained confirming that his order had been received and was being acted upon. For his actions in command of the close escort, and remaining at his post despite his serious wound, he was subsequently awarded the Victoria Cross.

The situation facing Commander Kinloch as he took command at

10.35 was far from clear, (see map, below). The convoy now steered 180° (due south), with *Obedient* and *Obdurate* some 3 miles (5.5 km) to the north and overhauling the merchantmen. *Orwell* closed from somewhat to the north-east, while *Onslow* made her way toward the head of the convoy from where she could 'home' Force 'R' using the fleet waveband. As the flotilla leader passed close to *Obedient*, Paddy Donovan, in the gunnery director up behind the bridge, had a grandstand view of the fires raging aboard *Onslow* and remembered *Obedient*'s crew cheering the battered destroyer as she steered to the head of the convoy.[7] *Achates* remained on station astern of the convoy, a little to the

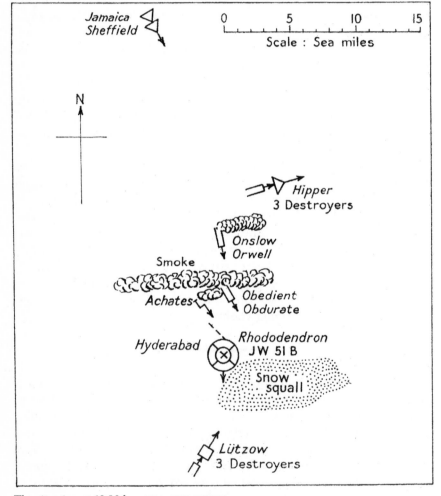

The situation at 10.30 hrs *(PRO. ADM. 234/369)*

66

west of *Obedient* and still laying smoke, while *Hipper* continued eastwards at 31 knots, although as a heavy snow squall now covered the area Kinloch had no real idea where the German cruiser was. To add to his problems *Rhododendron*, on the port quarter of the convoy, reported smoke to the south-west followed ten minutes later by a report of a large vessel bearing 160°, only 2 miles (3.2 km) off and steering north-east.[8] This was *Lützow*'s squadron, and had also been spotted by Lieutenant-Commander Marchant, now commanding *Onslow*:

> At a range of about 6000 yards [5486 m], on a bearing of green 40 [off the destroyer's starboard bow], silently slid into view the huge silhouette of the German pocket battleship *Lützow*. She was steering NNE. If, in our predicament, we could see her, surely she could see us and the . . . ships with us. So we simply stopped breathing and waited for the first broadside. But nothing happened! As quietly as she came into view she slid out – a ghost ship if ever there was. Many prayers winged aloft during those charged and tense minutes.[9]

A sudden desire for quiet prayer and contemplation seems also to have gripped the crew of *Rhododendron* at this point – a feeling which apparently did not extend to her captain, Lieutenant-Commander Sayers who apparently, so the scuttlebutt goes, ordered her single 4 in (101 mm) gun to open fire! The first lieutenant is said to have quickly checked the order and had a quiet word with the captain to the effect that they might be biting off a bit more than they could chew! In the event *Rhododendron* did not open fire and *Lützow* disappeared quietly back into the murk. While one cannot help but admire Sayers's spirit, it seems certain that letting sleeping battleships lie constituted the better part of valour on that occasion.

That morning *Lützow* and her three destroyers, *Theodor Riedel*, *Z30*, and *Z31*, made good progress north-eastwards toward the convoy. The pocket battleship made a better-than-expected 26 knots, *Kapitän zur See* Stange having authorised the temporary circumvention of the engines' operating limits.[10] At 09.30 muzzle flashes were seen from below the visible horizon, indicating the opening of *Admiral Hipper*'s attack, whereupon Stange considered launching the ship's aircraft for reconnaissance but decided against it, since much time would be lost recovering it. During the course of the morning Lieutenant-Commander Kaiser and *Z30*, in company with *Z31*, had been despatched in an attempt to locate the convoy but without success, and by 10.35 they had rejoined *Lützow*. At 10.42 a ship believed to be an enemy was in sight to port but was almost immediately obscured by the snow squall, which also blotted *Hipper* off from Commander Kinloch's view. By 10.45 *Lützow*'s radar picked up several targets within the snow squall, but still nothing was visible. *Kapitän zur See* Stange was now confronted by several problems. He presumed that the contacts in the squall would be the enemy convoy, but was not sure. Since he had no wish to get caught in the southward-moving squall himself it was necessary for him to manoeuvre his squadron into the best position to confirm the identity of the radar contacts, and if they turned out to be the merchantmen, make his attack. Stange opted to continue north-eastwards, pass ahead of the weather front, reduce speed to 15 knots and turn to run south eastwards along its edge, hoping for it to clear sufficiently to allow positive identification of the targets. As he manoeuvred for an attack position, in the back of his mind must have been the morning's message detailing *Lützow* to a further solo mission on completion of the attack on the convoy. This mission could only take place if the pocket battleship had at least half her ammunition and torpedoes available; therefore Stange would not have wished to waste either on indistinct targets. He could despatch one or more of his consorts to close on what he suspected would be the convoy, but decided against this course of action believing that an attack by *Lützow* would be jeopardised should his destroyers be intermingled with the enemy (to the north Vice-Admiral Kummetz kept his destroyers in close contact with *Hipper* for much the same reason).

Little had been heard from *Bramble* since departing the convoy on the 29th to search for stragglers, but she now made a dramatic but short-lived reappearance. Having no doubt seen the gunfire and set course for the convoy, she now approached from the north-east and at 10.39 sent her last message (received by *Hyderabad* only, and not passed on to the senior officer of the escort until some days later): 'One cruiser bearing 300°.'[11]

After disengaging from *Onslow*, *Admiral Hipper* continued eastwards before swinging in an arc to starboard to bring her back into contact with the convoy. At 10.42 as she came around to the south-west a ship appeared out of the gloom to port and was identified as a destroyer or corvette (see map B, p. 146). Since no German ship could be approaching from that direction *Hipper* opened fire on what was in fact the unfortunate *Bramble*. Having crippled the minesweeper Kummetz despatched *Friedrich Eckholdt* to finish her off. Little is known of this episode, except that *Obedient* noted an engagement between a small ship firing a single gun and a much larger ship, away to the north-east. *Bramble* was sunk with all hands, and evidently went down fighting.

Approaching 11.00 *Lützow* was steering 120° at 12 knots[12] and was spotted by *Obedient*, in company with *Obdurate* and *Orwell*, as the destroyers passed southward down the port side of the convoy (see map B, p. 146). As the destroyers conformed to the enemy's course and speed to keep themselves between the convoy and the pocket battleship, Commander Kinloch ordered *Achates* to join them. However, on being advised that *Achates'* speed was reduced to 20 knots by previously inflicted battle damage, he rescinded the order and signalled her to 'proceed to the head of the convoy and take *Onslow* under your orders.'[13] At 11.06 firing was heard and it was thought that *Lützow* had opened her attack, but no fall of shot could be seen. This was in fact *Hipper* racing back to the convoy at 31 knots on a course of 190° and a bearing almost exactly the same as *Lützow*, her approach therefore hidden from the British destroyers. What she had been firing at is something of a mystery as Kummetz reports her bombarding two destroyers to port,[14] yet there were no British ships in that area at the time. The only explanation appears to be that it may have been the luckless *Bramble* again, limping southwards.

Ordered to the head of the convoy, *Achates* emerged from her own smokescreen at 11.15, just as her adversary from earlier in the day arrived back on the scene. *Admiral Hipper* opened fire and the destroyer was immediately straddled. Lieutenant-Commander Johns took evasive action, increased speed and zigzagged in an attempt to upset the cruiser's gunnery.

Down below with the repair parties, Lieutenant Peyton-Jones felt the increase in speed and made his way up to the gunnery transmission station below the bridge and wheelhouse. As he arrived there was a heavy explosion and the ship shuddered from what must have been a direct hit. Going out on deck he could see no immediate signs of damage, but as he made for the bridge he was met by a white-faced young seaman sent to fetch him. Arriving first at the wheelhouse, he could see that the hit must have been to the bridge above, as the deckhead now bulged ominously downwards. In the wheelhouse, Coxswain Daniel Hall endeavoured to revive two telegraphsmen who lay wounded and in shock beside him. As the usual way up to the bridge had been wrecked, Peyton-Jones stepped out onto the port Oerlikon platform and clambered up the remains of an outside ladder. The bridge was a shambles of blackened twisted metal, with the remains of a few recognisable objects sticking grotesquely out of the wreckage. Where the compass platform had been, Lieutenant-Commander Johns, the officers, signalmen, lookouts and asdic operators who had been standing there were all killed, their remains 'mercifully unrecognisable'. Farther to the rear of the bridge the damage was less severe, but yet more bodies, some dead some wounded, lay scattered about. Yeoman Albert Taylor stumbled forward, dazed and in shock, but still able haltingly to tell Lieutenant Peyton-Jones of the recent exchange of signals with *Obedient.* However, a more immediate problem than the tactical situation intervened. In response to the last orders given, *Achates* steamed at 28 knots, circling to starboard under 20 degrees of wheel and with a consequent 20 degree list to port. The only way to communicate with the wheelhouse below was through a jagged hole in the deck and Peyton-Jones shouted to Hall to put the wheel amidships. He was much relieved to receive the coxwain's reply that the steering appeared to be undamaged. The destroyer slowly came around to a south-easterly course, and the heel to port decreased. The engine-room telegraph was not working however, and orders had to be passed down by word of mouth.[15]

As Lieutenant Peyton-Jones attempted to take stock of the situation shells exploded on either side of the destroyer, sending columns of water mushrooming skywards as *Hipper* tried once more to finish the job she had started that morning. Word was sent to the only gun now working, the aft main turret, to open fire, but the message never arrived, the messenger almost certainly having been killed *en route.* The view from the shattered remains of the bridge was severely restricted by thick smoke belching from a cordite fire which had broken out on 'B' gundeck immediately forward, so Peyton-Jones could only guess at who and where *Achates'* adversary might be. Shouting down to the wheelhouse for a sharp turn to port the first lieutenant heard and felt another loud explosion as the ship suffered another direct hit, while two near misses sent yet more shell fragments searing through her side. However as the destroyer came around into the wind, heavy seas shipped over the forecastle put out the fire on 'B' gundeck and, better able to see, Peyton-Jones peered toward the horizon for the next ripple of gun flashes. When they came he was relieved to see that *Hipper* was no longer firing at them.[16]

With Yeoman Taylor's help he was able to establish *Achates'* position. In the half-light *Rhododendron, Hyderabad,* and *Northern Gem* were just discernable shepherding the convoy southward. Away to the north-east a faster group, which it was assumed were the British destroyers, could just be made out, while to the north gunflashes still lit up the horizon. The tactical situation now was far from clear, but it did appear that whatever threat there was lay to the north; consequently Peyton-Jones decided to ignore his earlier orders to join *Onslow*, instead maintaining position astern of the convoy to recommence laying smoke – the only defence *Achates* was now in any condition to give to the merchantmen. As the black clouds rolled once more from the funnel, he conned the ship onto a broad weave across the stern of the convoy.[17]

1   PRO. ADM 234/492. Observers on the destroyers reported up to three hits on *Hipper* during this exchange, but there are no reports of hits at this time in the German records.
2   Ibid.
3   From a transcript of an interview taped by Lieutenant-Commander Marchant for the 17th Destroyer Flotilla Association, and used with the kind permission of Mrs Pamela Marchant.
4   PRO. ADM 234/492
5   Leading Stoker Walter Watkin, in correspondence with the author.
6   Ibid.
7   Lieutenant-Commander Donovan in conversation with the author.
8   *Hyderabad,* stationed on the starboard side of the convoy, had previously noticed two destroyers and a large ship crossing ahead from west to east, but again made no report.
9   Marchant interview, op. cit.
10 Stange, *Kapitän zur See* Lützow *War Diary*, Bundesarchiv.
11 PRO. ADM 199/73
12 Stange, op. cit.
13 PRO. ADM 234/492
14 Kummetz, Vice-Admiral Oskar *Diary of Operation* Regenbrogen, Bundesarchiv.
15 From the Memoir of Commander Loftus Peyton-Jones supplied to the author.
16 Ibid.
17 Ibid.

CHAPTER 6

'STEER FOR THE SOUND OF THE GUNS'

At 11.15 *Kapitän zur See* Stange altered course eastwards to 090° to take *Lützow* away from the snow squall, and out of the smokescreen laid by the convoy escorts. Gun flashes from *Hipper*'s engagement with *Achates* could be seen in the distance port side astern, and as there appeared to be no prospect of anything approaching a clear target in his present position, Stange made the decision to come around full circle, set course to link up with *Hipper* and attack in concert with the flagship. Starting at 11.26 Stange made his turn to starboard, subsequently increasing speed to 24 knots as he returned to the north-west.[1]

Shadowing *Lützow* in all these manoeuvres, the British destroyers *Obedient, Obdurate* and *Orwell* kept themselves between their menacing opponent and the convoy. It was now the turn of *Obedient* to find herself the target of accurate fire, Commander Kinloch initially being under the impression that *Lützow* had opened on her. It was, however, the ever-present *Admiral Hipper* away to the north-east. Having finished with *Achates* she shifted her fire, and at a range of 8500 yards (7760 m) strad-dled *Obedient*, putting the destroyer's wireless out of action and obliging Commander Kinloch to hand over direction (but not overall command) of the destroyers to Lieutenant-Commander Sclater of *Obdurate*.

Still wary of torpedo attack, *Hipper* altered away to starboard, coming on to course 360° (due north), Kummetz intending to come around shortly to drive on the convoy again. At 11.32, on the submarine frequency, the Vice-Admiral signalled to Narvik: 'Battle with protection forces. No cruisers with the convoy.'[2]

Conforming to instructions laid down by Captain Sherbrooke, as the range opened to *Hipper* the British destroyers altered to port to close on the convoy, (see map, p. 74).[3]

The battle had not gone entirely as Vice-Admiral Kummetz had planned, but this was probably not unexpected given the poor light

and complications with the weather, which must have been anticipated. Nevertheless, with the time at just after 11.30 the two powerful
German squadrons were undamaged, and coming together to brush
the three British destroyers remaining in action aside and fall upon the
merchant ships of the convoy.

———————————

Command in battle is inevitably a highly complex affair, but there is
one principle to which British armed forces are expected unfailingly
to adhere, a principle designed to clarify any and all situations which
might arise – 'When in doubt, steer for the sound of the guns.'

Having left the mystery echo behind, Rear-Admiral Burnett with
Force 'R' now put this principle into operation with a vengeance.
Heading due south at 31 knots, by 10.30 it was evident from continuing gunflashes on the horizon that a sustained engagement was in
progress. At this time an RDF contact was obtained on a vessel larger
than a destroyer, faster than a merchant vessel, and therefore necessarily an enemy. This contact, bearing 180°, was followed shortly by
contact with another large vessel bearing 140°, distance 30,000 yards
(27,432 m). Rear-Admiral Burnett altered to port to track the targets,
and at 10.54 when the second contact made a turn to the south-east,
he altered to conform. As the second target appeared to be moving
away from the scene, and the original target was in action and firing
to the eastward, at 11.12 Rear-Admiral Burnett altered course to 190°,
directly toward this engagement.[4] As observers on the rapidly
approaching British cruisers attempted to identify their target, at 11.28
the big warship altered to starboard, presenting her broadside to them.
Most observers in Force 'R' believed they were closing on *Lützow*,
though it was in fact *Admiral Hipper* turning away from her attack on
Obedient. (This incorrect identification is not too difficult to understand
given the poor visibility, augmented perhaps by the fact that the cruiser
Hipper was physically the larger of the two German heavy ships
present, despite *Lützow* being the more powerful pocket battleship
type.) At 11.30 Force 'R' also made a turn to starboard, and a minute
or so later, at a range of 16,000 yards, (14,630 m), Captain Storey gave
the order and *Sheffield* opened fire, followed rapidly by *Jamaica*.[5]

———————————

Midshipman Hutton, aboard *Jamaica*, heard the alarm sound with what
seemed to be 'extra urgency' at 9.10 that morning. Dashing to the

73

bridge he found the captain, navigating officer and others already at their posts in their anti-flash gear and tin hats. At his action station were massive pairs of binoculars, one mounted either side of the bridge, with pointers indicating to the director control tower any specific target which the captain wished to engage – 'a rather antiquated concept, but wonderful for seeing what was going on'.

As *Jamaica* raced along in line astern of *Sheffield* the young midshipman could not help but find the situation thrilling, while at the same time being aware that only a sketchy idea was to be had of what the two cruisers were speeding into. As Force 'R' rapidly closed on its target, Midshipman Hutton spotted the menacing shape of *Admiral Hipper* slide out of the Arctic gloom at 10,000 yards (9144 m) distance, and almost immediately they were in action: 'We were able to engage

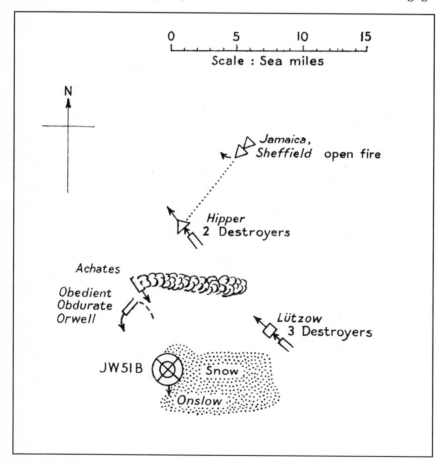

The situation at 11.30 hrs *(PRO. ADM. 234/369)*

her before she became aware of the two British cruisers. Good old fashioned stuff, the flash of our guns and within the relevant time of flight, one hoped the glow from a hit.' As *Hipper* and Force 'R' continued around on their turn to starboard, he recalled: 'our hurtling across *Hipper*'s bow, and she seemed massive bearing down on us at what was now about nine thousand yards [8229 m]'.[6]

On board *Admiral Hipper* there was consternation at this new attack. Absorbed by their engagements with the destroyers, an all-round RDF watch had not been maintained; consequently Kummetz had no idea of the British cruisers' presence until they opened fire from his starboard quarter.

Hipper was straddled by *Sheffield*'s first salvo and with the second suffered a direct hit to her No. 3 boiler room. This plunging shot struck *Hipper* as she heeled over to port while making her starboard turn, the shell entering her starboard side some 11 ft 6 in (3.5 m) below the waterline, and below the armoured belt around her hull (see diagram, p. 77). The shell sliced through a bunker oil tank before entering and detonating in the boiler room, which caught fire and began to fill with water topped with fuel oil from the ruptured tank. Incredibly, the only fatality was Engineering Mate Gunther Walter, who received severe head injuries and drowned. Also injured was Engineering Lance Corporal Heinz Hess, who was rescued and taken to a first-aid station. The fires were brought under some measure of control with the use of Ardexin* fire extinguishers, but with the influx of an estimated thousand tons of sea water into the ship, the boiler room had to be shut down. This also necessitated the shutting down of the cruiser's starboard main engine, and speed reduced to 28 knots as a consequence.

Meanwhile the engagement continued, and as *Sheffield* fired two further salvoes in quick succession, *Hipper* received two more hits, the first setting fire to her aircraft hangar amidships, the second entering her starboard side and tearing through the midship compartments causing a number of casualties, finally coming to rest against the inner wall of the hull on the port side, but incredibly failing to explode (see diagram, p. 77). *Hipper* returned fire but the columns of spray thrown up by near misses from *Sheffield* froze on contact with the instruments on her forward observation position, while the view from the rear observation position was cloaked by thick oily black smoke issuing

---

* The commercial name for a tetrachlorine carbon chemical. See also Chapter 8.

from her funnel as a consequence of the hit to the boiler room, aggravated by smoke from the burning hangar.[7] The result was that her usually accurate salvoes were ragged and wide of the mark. Josef Schmitz, control telephone officer for heavy artillery aboard *Admiral Hipper* during the battle, remembered: '*Hipper* had not shot for some time due to the change in sides [she had been engaging *Obedient* to port before making her starboard turn] . . . Nevertheless the [British] cruiser's fire was good and fast and *Hipper* received first hits. This threw *Hipper* into a state of uncertainty.'[8]

For Vice-Admiral Kummetz the situation had now changed dramatically.

> *Hipper* has been hit, the consequences of which cannot be fully assessed at the moment. Her hangar is on fire, but this is being controlled. Judging by the thick black smoke coming out of the funnel . . . which blocks any vision astern, it appears that the boiler has been hit. The incoming report of a blow in K3 and the breakdown of power station 3 confirm this assumption. *Hipper*'s ability for battle has been reduced. Time will tell the full impact of the blows. The enemy's type of ship, which has just appeared on the scene and bombarded *Hipper* from the north, has not yet been identified beyond doubt. According to the kind of shooting, the closeness of the impacts and their effect, it can only be a cruiser. If this is the case I am positioned between an enemy cruiser and the convoy destroyers in the south.
>
> I have to pull out of this unfavourable tactical situation, especially as it has become even more difficult to keep an overview of the overall situation due to the deteriorating visibility. Going down south, which would move me away from the cruiser and closer to the convoy would offer the possibility of a renewed convoy attack [but] cannot be considered due to the uncertain condition of *Hipper*. Neither can I release the destroyers close to *Hipper* to let them operate against the convoy on their own. I therefore decide to pull all armed forces to the west away from the battle area.[9]

As a result of his deliberations, at 11.37 Kummetz signalled to his squadron: 'Break off, turn away to the west.'[10]

Having been detached to finish off *Bramble*, 5th Destroyer Flotilla leader *Friedrich Eckholdt*, now in company with *Richard Beitzen*, had been attempting to rejoin *Hipper* from the north-east when the engagement with Force 'R' erupted.

Damage to *Admiral Hipper* from *Sheffield*'s first salvoes.

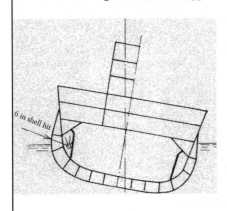

(a) 6 in (152 mm) shell causes severe damage to No. 3 boiler room as *Hipper* heels over to port (cross-section looking aft)

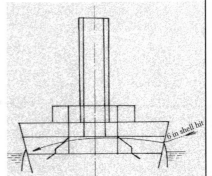

(b) 6 in (152 mm) shell enters starboard side, traverses midship compartments causing damage and casualties, but fails to explode (cross-section looking forward) (*Diagrams reproduced with permission from Bernard & Graefe Verlag, Bonn*)

Peering into the deepening gloom from *Eckholdt*'s bridge, Flotilla Commander Schemmel observed gunflashes and the dim shape of two warships ahead. Assuming that these were *Hipper* and *Z29*, Schemmel could not make out their target as the convoy should have been away to the south. At 11.42 he exchanged radio messages with the flagship:

'*Eckholdt* to *Hipper*. I can see a cruiser and destroyer at 300°, is that you?'

'*Eckholdt* to *Hipper*. In what direction to the convoy are you?'

'*Hipper* to *Eckholdt*. North of the convoy.'

Schemmel could see no other ships in the rapidly worsening light and sent a hurried reply: '*Eckholdt* to *Hipper*. You are bombarding me.'

Astern of the flotilla leader the awful truth dawned, and *Richard Beitzen* sent a hurried message: '*Beitzen* to *Eckholdt*. No. It's an English cruiser.'[11]

With Force 'R' shadowing *Hipper* around in a turn to starboard (see map B, p. 146), an urgent report was received on *Sheffield*'s bridge that a destroyer had been sighted fine on the port bow, at a range of some

4000 yards (3657 m) and closing fast. Captain Storey ordered the flag-ship's helm reversed hard to port, as presenting the cruiser's beam to the destroyer would make her a sitting target for a torpedo attack. As she swung round *Sheffield* engaged the destroyer, now fast approach-ing on her starboard bow, with all arms from her main 6 in (152 mm) down to her anti-aircraft pom-poms. Paying the price for her mistaken identification of the warships ahead of her, *Friedrich Eckholdt* was hit by *Sheffield*'s first salvo, heavily damaged by the third and was down by the stern, on fire, and a complete shambles when fire was checked after the sixteenth salvo.[12] Astern of *Sheffield, Jamaica* engaged *Richard Beitzen* but the German destroyer had better luck than her flotilla leader, turning away at speed to make her escape undamaged.

Closed up at action stations in *Sheffield*'s 'A' turret, Midshipman Twiddy could see nothing of what went on outside. As 'phone number', his only contact with the outside world was the telephone headset that he wore, through which came instructions from the 6 in director tower. The guns were fired automatically from the director, but the eighteen-man turret crew were responsible for loading shells and cordite, applying correct settings for training and elevation, setting fuses, and being prepared to operate all systems local to the guns should power fail or other malfunc-tions occur.

As Albert Twiddy recalled, the turret of a warship in battle is no place for the faint-hearted:

> My vivid memories during the action are of excessive vibration as the ship was making best speed, and the acrid smell of burning cordite. The loud crashes as the bows ploughed into the heavy seas, the continuous noise of activity within the turret as the machinery for shell and cordite handling began providing the ammunition to the guns, and men in the guns crews applying themselves to the task, shouting their reports to be heard above all else that was going on. I was concentrating on listening to the orders being received through my headphones, and ensuring as best I could that I understood them, and relaying them as correctly as I knew how to those in the turret who had to obey them. I do remember well that at some point during the action when the elevation of the guns was as low, or even lower than ever I had experienced in practice and training, when the gun breeches were high enough to make the ramming of shells and cordite more difficult, the order was received to set fuses 2 at delay, and 1 at non-delay. [This enabled part of the salvo

to explode immediately on contact, whereas the remainder would penetrate armour before exploding, to cause maximum damage. Fuses were in the nose of the shells and required setting manually before being loaded.] . . . The seriousness of the situation became apparent when the next instruction, 'Stand by to Ram', was given. We were just so close to the enemy that this would have been the Coup de Grâce, though how we would have fared is certainly open to conjecture . . . However, the order was very quickly 'belayed', and firing ceased temporarily. The quiet that descended was as dramatic as had been the noise, and speculation as to what had happened was rife.

As I recall we were shortly informed by ship's broadcast that we had attacked and destroyed an enemy vessel, and for some reason which I cannot now explain, a number of us were permitted to leave the turret and go out on deck to see this dark grey wreck of a vessel a short distance away, some 2–300 yards [180–275 m] at most, listing over with her hull exposed and with fires burning at various points along her deck, so slowly passing down our ship's side. The upper deck short-range weapons raked the burning deck with gunfire as she drifted astern of us into the darkness and oblivion. I cannot remember seeing any movement nor signs of life on board, nor could I understand why this was so . . . It was an eerie and to my mind ghostly vision, unreal, as though in a black-and-white film, but the flames already dying as they were, seemed to illustrate the submissive though reluctant finality of a gallant foe.[13]

Friedrich Eckholdt went down with all hands.

———

Kummetz must have been aware that the destroyer had run into the British cruisers, and being unable to contact her after 11.45 must have guessed her fate. With this in mind and with *Hipper* damaged, moreover mindful of his strict instructions not to risk the heavy ships, at 11.49 the vice-admiral signalled to both squadrons: 'Break off battle, turn off west.'[14]

———

Aboard *Obdurate*, *Obedient* and *Orwell*, the sight and sound of Rear-Admiral Burnett's guns to the north-east was a godsend. They had been laying smoke to cover the convoy and knew he was on his way, but had only a sketchy idea of where or when he would arrive. Despite the smoke, at 11.42 *Lützow* finally caught a glimpse of her quarry and opened on the merchantmen with her secondary armament, straddling the freighter *Calobre*, peppering her with splinters and forcing her to drop out of line and transfer the convoy vice-commodore to *Daldorch*.[15] The convoy made an emergency turn to course 225°, while the British destroyers came around to the eastward to cover it with smoke and open fire on the German pocket battleship, although all their shots fell short. In reply one of the *Lützow* squadron destroyers, in all probability *Z30*, also opened fire. Johann Hengel was at his action station at the aft radio station and remembers:

> My service started at 08.00 and went on until 12.00. During this time we came to a full-scale alert, everybody was at battle stations . . . At approximately 11.00 hours we had our first battle contact. I remember this exactly because at the time I briefly left the radio station. Dawn was breaking, one could see the visible horizon very well.* Our ship's artillery as well as our fourfold torpedo came into action.[16]

None of *Z30*'s shells or torpedoes found their target, and following one broadside with her main armament, *Lützow* also ceased firing. At 11.45 she made a turn to port, coming onto course 290° to join up with *Hipper*.

Shortly thereafter Commander Kinloch sighted *Admiral Hipper* and her two destroyers 4–5 miles (7.5–9.2 km) to the north, on a south-westerly course. The British destroyers turned together to the north-west and with *Obdurate* leading, steered to place themselves between the convoy and this new enemy. By this time, however, *Lützow* was rapidly closing the distance to *Hipper* and with her secondary armament opened an accurate fire on the British destroyers, to which they replied. At 12.00 *Lützow*'s main armament joined in, and *Obdurate* immediately suffered damage from a near miss.

◆

The twenty-year-old officers' cook aboard *Orwell*, Smith Belford, witnessed the duel between the destroyers and their fearsome opponent from his action station at ammunition supply for the destroyer's 'Y' turret. Ammunition was stored under the captain's cabin (not to be confused with the captain's day cabin under the

---

* To reconcile this with *Kapitän zur See* Stange's assertion that visibility was extremely poor, it should be remembered that the convoy, and the weather front covering it, was at this time on the western or 'dark' side of the *Lützow* squadron as they headed north-westwards.

bridge), sent up via two chutes then pushed by hand up a slide to the turret. Standing on the upper deck, Belford saw in the distance the telltale ripples of flame as *Lützow* opened fire and the first salvo screeching over the speeding destroyer. He remembered Lieutenant-Commander Austen ordering 'Astern!' The abrupt change in pace evidently upset the pocket battleship's gunnery as the next salvo fell just ahead, where *Orwell* would have been.[17] *Lützow* was also considerably hindered by the freezing up of her navigation periscopes and target instruments.

As both the *Hipper* and *Lützow* squadrons continued off to westward, the British destroyers again fell back to cover the convoy.

Bearing round in a wide loop to port, having engaged *Eckholdt* and *Beitzen*, at 11.54 Force 'R' altered course to westward and at 12.15 obtained an RDF contact on a large ship bearing 230°. This was *Hipper* retiring from the battle, and was followed at 12.23 by the sighting of two destroyers to the south at some 8000 yards (7315 m) distance. These were almost certainly *Richard Beitzen* and *Z29*, and they were in a good position from which to launch a torpedo attack. Rear-Admiral Burnett altered course southward to engage them, however in the director control tower above *Sheffield*'s bridge, observers had spotted *Lützow* beyond the destroyers at a range of some 17,000 yards (15,544 m). Closing to 14,000 yards, (12,801 m), *Sheffield* and *Jamaica* opened fire on the pocket battleship at 12.29. *Lützow* replied immediately with main and secondary armament, and was joined a few moments later by *Admiral Hipper*. Observation positions on the German flagship were now clear of ice and smoke, and within minutes her salvos straddled the British cruisers. Force 'R' was now coming under fire from *Lützow* to the south and *Hipper* to the west, and had also to watch for torpedo attacks from the destroyers.[18] In view of this Rear-Admiral Burnett altered away to the northward, and by 12.36 the battle was over. *Jamaica* claimed one hit on *Lützow* but there are no reports of damage to the pocket battleship in the German records.

Rear-Admiral Burnett maintained contact with the withdrawing German forces until 13.45 when radar contact was lost. He first swept south then north to ensure that the enemy were not doubling back, then returned to cover the convoy, which he had still not seen, and of whose position he was still very uncertain.

As the drama of the battle was being played out, another drama, and one that was to have disastrous consequences for the *Kriegsmarine*, was just beginning. Observing the battle from some distance, at 11.45 (just as Force 'R' engaged *Hipper* and *Eckholdt* in quick succession), *Kapitän-leutnant* Herschelb of *U354* despatched a curiously worded message to Admiral Kluber in Narvik – a message destined to be dramatically misunderstood by the German high command: 'Watching from this locality the battle has reached its climax. I can see only red.'[19]

1   Stange, *Kapitän zur See* Lützow *War Diary*, Bundesarchiv. Translated from the original German.
2   Kummetz, Vice-Admiral Oskar *Diary of Operation* Regenbogen, Bundesarchiv. Translated from the original German.
3   PRO. ADM 234/369
4   PRO. ADM 1/14217
5   There is some disagreement as to the range at which *Sheffield* opened fire, as neither she or *Jamaica* were using RDF spotting observations (such was the delicacy of the equipment at this time that *Jamaica*'s forward RDF was put out of action by vibration from her own first salvo). Admiral Tovey later stated that he thought the range might more likely have been about 13,000 yards (11,887 m). Distinguishing the fall of shot from the two cruisers presented no difficulty as *Jamaica* fired eight tracer per salvo, and *Sheffield* two, subsequently amended to four.
6   Captain Michael Hutton, in correspondence with the author.
7   Brennecke, Jochen *Eismeer, Atlantik, Ostee* (Arctic Ocean, Atlantic, Baltic Sea). A history of the wartime career of *Admiral Hipper*, published in Germany, which draws upon German reports and the experiences of German veterans. Made available to the author by *Herr* Josef Schmitz, control telephone officer for heavy artillery aboard *Admiral Hipper* during the battle.
8   Josef Schmitz, in correspondence with the author.
9   Kummetz, op. cit.
10 Ibid. Several German accounts of the battle state that at this critical time Vice-Admiral Kummetz received a morse code message from Admiral Kluber stating baldly 'no unnecessary risk'. Admiral Kluber apparently intended only to underline the *Führer*'s overall strategy, not actions when in contact with the enemy. However even if this was Kluber's intention, Kummetz could hardly be expected to grasp such subtle nuances from a three-word message while under fire. Vice-Admiral Kummetz makes no direct reference to this message in his report of the battle but see p. 104 and note, 10 p. 111.
11 Ibid.
12 PRO. ADM 1/14217
13 Lieutenant-Commander Albert Twiddy, in correspondence with the author.
14 Kummetz, op. cit.
15 Stange, op. cit.
16 Johann Hengel, in correspondence with the author.
17 Smith Belford, in conversation with the author.
18 PRO. ADM 1/14217
19 Kummetz, op. cit.

Robert St Vincent Sherbrooke, VC, DSO, RN, Captain (D) 17th Destroyer Flotilla, awarded the Victoria Cross for his actions in command of the *JW51B* close escort. Captain Sherbrooke suffered serious injuries in the action. (*Photo: IWM HU1920*)

British destroyer HMS *Onslow*, leader, 17th Destroyer Flotilla. (*Photo: IWM A9285*)

Direct hit to *Onslow*'s funnel, one of three 8 in shell hits sustained while engaging *Admiral Hipper*. Splinters from this explosion showered the bridge, badly wounding Captain Sherbrooke. (*Photo: IWM. MH10406*)

Vice-Admiral Oskar Kummetz. His plan for Operation *Regenbogen* was a good one, but the German high command, principally Hitler himself, placed the admiral under crippling restrictions. (*Photo: IWM A 14900*)

Grand Admiral Erich Raeder. He held the post of C-in-C German navy from 1928, but felt compelled to resign at his meeting with Hitler of 6 January 1943, called as a result of the Battle of the Barents Sea. (*Photo: IWM A14906*)

Vice-Admiral Kummetz's flagship for the attack on convoy *JW51B*, the heavy cruiser *Admiral Hipper*, at anchor in Trondheim Fjord.

Kapitän zur See Hans Hartmann captained *Admiral Hipper* for the Barents Sea action – pictured later as a vice-admiral. (*Photo: Mr Klaus Hartman*)

With *Admiral Hipper* spending much of her time in Norwegian waters, concerts, with entertainers from home, made a welcome break. Josef Schmitz is pictured above and to the right of the singer's head, looking towards the left of the picture.

Admiral Hipper, Division VII, weapons technicians for artillery, anti-aircraft guns, torpedoes and ammunition. Four officers and approximately ninety crew.

British destroyer HMS *Obedient.* (*Photo: IWM A17864*)

Rear-Admiral Robert Burnett, C-in-C Force 'R', comprising the light cruisers *Sheffield* and *Jamaica.* (*Photo: IWM FLM1225*)

British light cruiser HMS *Sheffield*, Rear-Admiral Burnett's flagship, Force 'R' *(Photo: IWM A13970)*

British light cruiser HMS *Jamaica*, a brand-new ship – the Battle of the Barents Sea was her first action *(Photo: IWM A30157)*

German Maasz Class destroyer *Richard Beitzen*. This ship had a lucky escape while in company with her sister vessel and flotilla leader *Friedrich Eckholdt*. In poor visibility they mistook *Sheffield* for *Admiral Hipper*, and in the ensuing engagement *Friedrich Eckholdt* was sunk with all hands. (*Photo: IWM HU1051*)

British destroyer HMS *Achates*, sunk by *Admiral Hipper* while laying a smoke screen to cover the convoy. (*Photo: IWM FL51*)

British minesweeper HMS *Bramble*. Detached from the convoy to search for stragglers, she strayed across the path of *Admiral Hipper* and was sunk with all hands. (*Photo: IWM A6338*)

Royal Indian Navy corvette *Hyderabad*. Finding herself in position to make several important enemy sightings, she failed to pass most of them on. (*Photo: IWM FL 22671*)

CHAPTER 7

'ROLL OUT THE BARREL'

By the time *Hipper* had switched her fire to *Obedient*, the situation aboard *Achates* was less than encouraging. Chief Engineer Peter Wright, his head and shoulders poking up over the starboard edge of the wrecked bridge, reported to Lieutenant Peyton-Jones that the ship had taken a direct hit just below. The shell had torn a gaping hole in the port side before exploding in the seamen's bathroom, putting the nearby gunnery transmission station out of action and killing most of its crew. The explosion also fractured the after bulkhead of compartments already flooded earlier in the day, and extended the area of hull damage along the port side of the forecastle. A huge hole had been made in the ship's side abreast No. 2 boiler room, which had to be closed down and abandoned. Light and power in many parts of the ship had failed, and casualties had been severe. Decks and passageways were encumbered with the dead and wounded, but of James MacFarlane, the ship's doctor, there was no sign. It was assumed that he had been blown over the side as he journeyed between first-aid stations established at either end of the ship. Lieutenant Peyton-Jones ordered the crew to fall out from action stations, and for all available hands to assist Peter Wright in his efforts to restore what services he could and limit further flooding.[1]

By now *Achates* had taken on a 15° list to port, and being down by the head became difficult to steer. Nevertheless, with the aid of a boat's compass in the wheelhouse, it was possible to maintain a zigzag course across the stern of the convoy while laying a smokescreen; however, speed had reduced to 12 knots. Gun flashes could still be seen to the north and north-west, and at 11.45 a visual signal was flashed to *Hyderabad* to ask if the smokescreen was still effective. The reply was that it was 'most useful'.[2]

As time passed the list slowly increased, and as it did so more and more holes, as yet unplugged, sank below the water line. Eventually, at 13.00, Peter Wright reported to Peyton-Jones that, although the struggle still went on to save the ship, it was no longer possible to maintain steam in the only remaining boiler. Smoke stopped belching from the funnel, and *Achates* wallowed to a halt some 3 miles (4.8 km) on the starboard quarter of the convoy. The two men discussed the possibility of arranging a tow, and Wright went off to make preparations. Sadly, that was the last that Peyton-Jones saw of the Chief Engineer.[3]

On a salvaged box lamp, Yeoman Albert Taylor called up the nearest escort, the trawler *Northern Gem*, signalling 'Not under control. Please stand by me', adding a request to be taken in tow. However, this proved to be impractical with the existing degree of list, and Peyton-Jones had no option but to issue instructions to launch boats and carley floats, and get the wounded and everyone else onto the upper deck. *Northern Gem*'s skipper, Lieutenant Aisthorpe, later explained that the message flashed on the box lamp had been so difficult to read in the poor light that he half-thought that it might be transmitted by an enemy destroyer. As *Northern Gem* slowly approached, *Achates* started to roll slowly onto her port side, Peyton-Jones and Yeoman Taylor having to climb over the edge of the bridge onto the side of the wheelhouse, hauling crewmen up out of the wheelhouse passage, now at their feet, as they did so. The ship lay completely on her beam ends, with water pouring through ventilator outlets, doors, hatches, and the horizontal funnels. Lieutenant Peyton-Jones had time to hang his binoculars neatly on a convenient projection before the ship capsized completely, and the men found themselves in the freezing Arctic waters. As he struck out to get clear of the ship, Peyton-Jones looked back and saw her stern pointing skywards as she slowly disappeared.[4]

Achates sank at around 13.00, her position approximately 73°03' N, 30°42' E.

A good number of rafts and carley floats had been launched from the ship, and the First Lieutenant swam to one and climbed on, his chief concern now being that *Northern Gem* might have trouble locating them in the gathering darkness. The floats were provided with a flashing light for just such an emergency, and Peyton-Jones held it aloft for several minutes, thanking Providence that it was functioning correctly. Attracted by the light and his calls, some fifteen men gathered around the float, including Coxswain Daniel Hall. Wounded men, and those who seemed most distressed, were manhandled onto the float, and Peyton-Jones told them that *Northern Gem* was on her way. A suggestion was made that a sing-song would keep up their spirits, and they began to sing, a little uncertainly at first, the popular pub anthem 'Roll out the Barrel'. This was taken up by others in the water around them, and whether it helped them or not, it is on record as having amazed and inspired their rescuers.[5]

As *Northern Gem* approached, members of her crew climbed out onto the trawler's rubbing strake or were clinging to rescue nets which hung over the gunwale, ready to pull survivors aboard. Without this assistance, few could have hauled themselves up the trawler's side to safety. As it was, some, wounded, exhausted, and suffering the debilitating effects of hypothermia, could carry on no longer even with rescue so close, and drifted away. Peyton-Jones and his companions paddled towards *Northern Gem* and someone threw them a line, which was made fast to the float. Unfortunately, in the urgency of the moment, everyone crowded to one side and the float capsized, throwing them all back into the sea. The trawler's crew struggled manfully to get survivors inboard but it was no easy task, the men in the water being weighed down as they were with bulky sodden clothing, and able to do little to help themselves. Lieutenant Peyton-Jones became aware of increasing numbness, and climbed back onto the empty carley float, pulling off his heavy sheepskin jacket and seaboots. Another survivor appeared and was helped onto the float. By now most of the swimmers had been rescued, and someone hauled the float back alongside while a member of *Northern Gem*'s crew hoisted Peyton-Jones's companion aboard on a bowline. The lieutenant was suddenly gripped by an overpowering feeling that if he did not get off the float now he never would, and stepping on to the side of the rolling and plunging raft, he leapt to hook his elbows over the trawler's gunwale, where willing hands grabbed him and deposited him in a heap on the deck.[6]

Referring to the part played by *Achates* in the battle, the C-in-C Home Fleet, Admiral Tovey, later remarked:

> I consider the action of Lieut. Commander A.H.T. Johns, RN, and subsequently Lieutenant L.E. Peyton-Jones, RN, to have been gallant in the extreme. They only had one idea, to give what protection they could to the convoy, and this they continued to do up to the moment of sinking. The behaviour of all officers and ratings was magnificent.

The admiral also highly commended Lieutenant Aisthorpe, RNR, for the 'courageous and seamanlike handling of the *Northern Gem*', which resulted in the rescue of so many survivors.[7]

The danger from further attack having passed, at 14.45 the convoy altered to 110°, back on course for Murmansk, and at 20.15 *Obedient* closed with *Northern Gem* to hear for the first time of the sinking of *Achates*. The trawler was fitted out as a rescue ship, and had bunks, blankets and dry kit for the destroyer's eighty-one survivors, but she had no doctor. It was decided that when *Northern Gem* caught up with the convoy, *Obdurate* should transfer her medical officer to the trawler.

Obedient sighted two ships at 20.47, bearing 180°, and made an enemy report, but this was cancelled when they were identified as two stragglers returning to the convoy.

Like *Achates*, flotilla leader *Onslow* had taken a severe pounding. As she took station at the head of the convoy following her engagement with *Hipper*, flames and smoke belched from her forecastle and beneath 'B' turret. The engine room still produced a monumental smoke screen which occasionally blew forward over the bridge, compounded by passing through a very effective smoke screen being laid by the convoy. Add to this steam issuing from escape pipes with such a roar that it was impossible to hear anyone speak, and the destroyer presented a spectacle which Dante would have recognised instantly.

The worst fire was in the petty officers' mess under 'B' turret, and the heat caused fires to break out in the chief petty officers' (CPOs') mess just aft. This had been taken over by the surgeon lieutenant, who attended to casualties there, and in the sick bay and the sick bay flat, under extremely difficult conditions. Finally, smoke and danger of the fire spreading made conditions in the CPOs' mess impossible, and it was decided to move all casualties aft.[8]

By 14.00 the fires were thankfully under control, and by 14.30 they were all out, but by now the ship had developed a 10° list to port. By flooding No. 7 oil tank this was reduced to 6°, but the large amount of water used to douse the fires brought it back to 10°. The forward shell room was flooded as a consequence, and the ship brought back on to an even keel. The sea was now relatively calm, and as water only entered through the hole in the torpedomen's messdeck when the ship rolled to port, it was possible by pumping to keep the height of the water down to 2 ft (0.61 m).[9]

As a fighting unit *Onslow* was now of little use; her ASDIC, RDF and forward guns were all out of action, and should the weather worsen she would be in grave danger of foundering. As a consequence, Lieutenant-Commander Marchant requested that she be allowed to proceed independently to the Kola Inlet, and Commander Kinloch agreed. At 19.30 *Onslow* was detached and given the 20.00 course and speed of the convoy, which she was to pass to Home Fleet Operational when 50 miles (80 km) clear. She arrived at Kola at 08.30 on 1 January and proceeded to Vaenga Pier to disembark her wounded, arriving there at noon.

On receipt of reports of the action on the 31st, C-in-C Home Fleet put to sea with the battleships *Howe* and *King George V* (flagship), the cruiser *Bermuda* and six destroyers, in case it should prove possible to catch the German battle group at sea. He also detached Rear-Admiral Hamilton with the cruisers *Kent* and *Berwick* to cover westbound convoy *RA51*. The battle fleet cruised to the west of Bear Island until 3 January (see map D, p. 148), then, being sure that the threat from German surface units had passed, returned to Scapa Flow followed on the 4th by Rear-Admiral Hamilton's cruisers.

For the convoy, the first day of January 1943 saw them making slow progress through weather which had been deteriorating for most of the night. With heavy seas and winds approaching gale force, at around 07.30 *Northern Gem*, with Lieutenant Aisthorpe himself taking the helm, edged toward *Obdurate*'s port quarter in order to transfer the doctor from the destroyer. Both ships yawed, rolled and pitched badly, but Lieutenant Aisthorpe skilfully closed the gap to around 10 ft (3.04 m). As the decks of the two ships rose and fell, the gap widened and narrowed but, calling upon all his exceptional seamanship, Aisthorpe judged the moment to nudge the destroyer's well-fendered side and the medical officer, Lieutenant Maurice Hood, bravely leapt the 8 ft (2.4 m) down to the trawler's deck. The difficult and dangerous manoeuvre had taken some two hours to complete, but once below, the doctor immediately set to work. As the storm continued, both he and those assisting him had to be anchored around the waist by two men each, enabling them to keep both hands free to minister to the injured as the tiny trawler corkscrewed around in the heavy seas.[10]

At 11.00 the convoy altered course to 185°, the noon position being 71°30' N, 38°24' E, at which time *Vizalma* and *Chester Valley* also made a welcome reappearance. With the wind blowing a lusty force 7, *Executive* began to fall astern due to excessive rolling and fears for her deck cargo, but by 23.00 the wind had dropped to force 2, and course was altered to 226° for the approach to Kola. At first light on 2 January land was sighted ahead, and at 10.15 the convoy altered north-westwards to 310° for entry into the inlet. *Calobre* had dropped astern during the night; otherwise all merchant ships were present and accounted for. As the White Sea had not yet frozen, the convoy re-formed into three columns, the starboard column departing at 13.00 to proceed down the coast to Archangel.

Close as the convoy was to its destination, a drama or two remained to be played out. Twice during the afternoon air-raid warnings were given, although mercifully no enemy planes appeared. At 17.40 Kildin Island on the approach to Kola was sighted, and *Obedient*, assisted by *Rhododendron*, led round to starboard to join up with the pilot vessel. Almost immediately *Ballot* went aground, and after the rest of the convoy had been shepherded into position, *Orwell* was detached to try and tow her free. Despite the best efforts of the destroyer, assisted by two Russian tugs through the night, as the morning of 3 January dawned *Ballot* remained firmly aground. Having almost completed the hazardous journey, the twenty-year-old veteran finally had to be abandoned within sight of port; nevertheless lighters subsequently removed her invaluable cargo.

From the early hours of the morning of the 3rd *Obedient*, *Rhododendron* and *Hyderabad* carried out anti-submarine patrols until finally, between 05.00 and 09.00, all merchant ships except *Calobre*, *Vermont* and *Pontfield* entered harbour. *Obedient* located *Vermont* anchored in the Kildin Straits, and in leading her to harbour was joined by *Vizalma*, which had been sent to find *Calobre* and was escorting her in. During a morning of heightened tension caused by more air-raid warnings, *Orwell* finally tracked down *Pontfield* which had also gone aground but was refloated by a Russian tug and towed safely down the inlet.

With the ships berthed, the men who had fought them through at last had a little time to themselves. Walter Watkin visited *Onslow*'s injured chief stoker, whom he had stopped from sliding into the sea, and Lieutenant Peyton-Jones called in on *Achates*' wounded, who had been transferred ashore. Sadly he found conditions in the hospital to be 'primitive'; nevertheless the two Royal Navy doctors on hand, joined by *Obdurate*'s Lieutenant Hood, struggled to cope under difficult circumstances.

During a previous visit to Murmansk, Peyton-Jones had attempted to requisition a particularly fine pair of Arctic gloves, but his request was firmly refused by the Base Supply Officer who ruled that they were for survivors only. Now that he qualified in all respects, he was glad to be able to obtain a pair of the gloves, with temperatures capable of plunging to –50°C.[11]

It was decided that most of *Achates*' survivors, including Lieutenant Peyton-Jones, and the more seriously wounded, including Captain Sherbrooke, should be taken home as soon as possible in *Obedient*. The destroyer sailed from Murmansk on 11 January and arrived at Scapa Flow five days later to refuel and transfer the wounded to a hospital ship. Peyton-Jones, and those survivors from *Achates* who were not wounded, carried on to Leith in *Obedient*, where buses were waiting on the jetty to take them on the next stage of their journeys home. With his shipmates mustered on the quayside, Lieutenant Peyton-Jones said a last few words, then shook each by the hand as they filed away. *Achates* had been a happy ship, and it was a moving moment, the end of a commission which all the survivors would have good reason to remember.

For Midshipman Albert Twiddy in *Sheffield*, not yet eighteen years old, the abiding memory of this, his first action, was the burning wreck of *Friedrich Eckholdt* – a brief moment which brought home the stark reality of war and the death of a ship and her crew, and which has remained a vivid image in his mind ever since. No doubt echoing the thoughts of many of those on both sides who survived, he recalls the last few hours of 1942 disappearing with only the feeling that God had spared his ship, his shipmates and himself on this occasion.

1   Memoir of Commander Loftus Peyton-Jones, as supplied to the author.
2   PRO. ADM 234/492
3   Peyton-Jones, op. cit.
4   Ibid.
5   Ibid.
6   Ibid.
7   PRO. ADM 234/369
8   PRO. ADM 234/492
9   Ibid.
10   Peyton-Jones, op. cit.
11   Ibid.

CHAPTER 8

SEEING RED

At 11.45, as *Sheffield* switched from her attack on *Hipper* to engage *Friedrich Eckholdt*, Admiral Kluber in Narvik despatched another message to Vice-Admiral Kummetz: 'Most immediate. Return passage at increased speed. Presence of 2 enemy cruisers in the Murmansk area confirmed. These include *Jamaica*'.[1]

So the German high command maintained its apparently relentless pressure to ensure that the commander at sea jumped at the sight of his own shadow. Vice-Admiral Kummetz received this message at 12.55, by which time he had already disengaged and was returning to Altenfjord, but the state of mind of the naval high command is clear, the message having been despatched while the engagement was still in progress. The *Kriegsmarine* had in action a battle group which, even separated into two squadrons, had the firepower to expect to be able to take on two light cruisers and five destroyers (which would also be separated, at least at the commencement of any action), and emerge victorious. Had the German high command been a little more aggressive they would surely have realised that they had been presented with a golden opportunity to inflict a significant defeat on their enemy's naval forces, plus the destruction of a convoy. They could not, however, achieve these great things without expecting damage of one sort or another to their heavy ships – but this desire to avoid damage to the big ships had become an obsession with Hitler. This obsession made itself felt down through the chain of command to the extent that the message quoted above, while rightly informing the commander at sea of the presence of two enemy cruisers in his area of operations, falls just short of ordering him to abandon his assault, regardless of the situation at sea, and betrays a tone approaching panic which is entirely inappropriate to the situation.

Withdrawing westward and believing *Sheffield* and *Jamaica* still to be in hot pursuit, Kummetz opted to cancel *Aurora*, *Lützow*'s solo operation, and at 12.33 sent a message to Narvik on the submarine frequency: 'No communication with *Eckholdt*. Enemy shadowers with formation. Not possible to detach *Lützow*.'[2]

Having despatched this message Kummetz took the understandable, but as later events were to show critical, decision to maintain complete radio silence during the return to Altenfjord due to continuing uncertainty as to the extent of *Hipper*'s damage and a desire not to give away the battle group's position.[3]

As mentioned, when *Sheffield*'s 6 in (152 mm) shell detonated in the German flagship's No. 3 boiler room a serious fire broke out, and tons of seawater plus fuel oil from a ruptured tank rapidly entered. As a result of the flooding, *Hipper* was down by the bows, and to restore her trim Second Boiler Engineer Dr (Eng.) von Pawel and Engineer Officer *Fregattenkapitän* (Eng.) Schafer arranged to pump fuel aft from the forepeak through oil transfer pipes which had to be laid through the steering compartment.[4]

After thirteen minutes it became necessary to shut down the boilers and abandon No. 3 boiler room, but temporary repairs were effected, the fire brought under control and the room pumped out. Despite the efforts of the damage-control parties, working in extremely difficult conditions, water and oil continued to enter and the room was again abandoned, necessitating the shutting down of the starboard main engine. At 12.18 the level of water and oil in No. 3 boiler room reached approximately 6 ft (1.83 m), and began to flood the adjacent No. 2 boiler room through leaks around the bulkhead glands for the interconnecting piping system between the two rooms. Desperate efforts were made to keep No. 2 boiler room in operation but water entered the boilers, causing cracks in the superheater tubes, and as a result fires in the boilers were extinguished, necessitating the shutting down of the port main engine – and a consequent reduction in speed to 15 knots. Engineers worked on in No. 2 boiler room and shortly after 18.00 their efforts were rewarded when sufficient pressure was raised on one boiler for speed to be increased to 18 knots, and maintained for the remainder of the voyage to Altenfjord.

The situation in the boiler rooms having been stabilised, the surrounding area was ventilated for three hours to enable those off watch to rest and get some sleep in nearby rooms. Despite the ventilation a number of crewmen suffered cramps, vomiting and shortness of breath, some coughing up a bloody foam, some becoming unconscious. Dr Martin Goeder, the ship's medical officer, diagnosed poisoning from Ardexin fumes, which proved to be extremely persistent despite the ventilation. This may have been due to leaking storage units (although they had been thoroughly checked), damaged as a result of vibration from the shell explosion, or from the firing of *Hipper*'s own guns. For the affected crewmen Dr Goeder prescribed medication for blood circulation, plus oxygen to be administered as

101

required for breathing difficulties. In a number of cases further treatment, requiring bleeding of 100 to 250 ccm, followed by the infusion of a physiological salt solution of 500 to 1000 ccm with a 100 ccm glucose solution, was used. In one case chloral hydrate as a clyster was administered, dissolved in glucose.[5]

Narvik ordered U-boats in the battle area to search for wreckage, and in particular to attempt to locate *Friedrich Eckholdt*. At 18.52 *U354* reported 'heavy artillery fire' at a distance of 10 miles (18.4 km), which, as the action was by then over, seems in all probability to have been ammunition aboard the German destroyer exploding as she tore herself apart.

At 02.45 on the morning of 1 January Kummetz received the following message from Kluber in Narvik, which gives some hint of the pressure for news of the operation emanating from much higher up the German chain of command: 'Emergency. Request brief preliminary survey by w/t of successes and situation, even before sending short report.'[6]

Kummetz coded his reply while at sea but declined to send it until the battle group had entered Lopphavet Sound, in order not to give any clues as to which route would be used for their return. As it was, *Hipper* was spotted by the British submarine *Graph* shortly after 01.00 on the 1st, but she was too far away to make an attack (see map D, p. 148). (Some three hours later *Graph* reported unsuccessfully attacking two enemy destroyers, one apparently in tow of the other, although there are no indications of serious battle damage to any of the remaining five German destroyers from the Barents Sea action, and Vice-Admiral Kummetz makes no mention of any problems in his report.) By 04.10, with the battle group safely in the fjords the Vice-Admiral despatched his message:

> 31.12 from 0230 hours onwards 5-Fl [5th Flotilla] reconnaissance strip Qu.4196 AC to 4939, cruisers behind it. *Hipper* convoy 0740hrs Qu.4395 sighted. Alarm. *Eckholdt* contact holder. Artillery battle *Hipper* with guarding destroyers, in the end cruisers, at first not recognised as such though. *Hipper*, 3 destroyers north, *Lützow*, 3 destroyers south, convoy. *Lützow* and various destroyers also in artillery battles. *Hipper* damaged 3 destroyers, 1 further probably sunk. *Eckholdt* was hit by cruiser artillery during sinking of this destroyer. Due to difficult enemy position and onset of darkness, assistance [to *Eckholdt*] no longer

possible without a high risk to the formation. Formation withdrawn westwards. At first enemy contact holders on both sides. *Hipper* suffered one full blow to K.3 from cruiser artillery. Due to overflow K.2 shut down . . . One blow to hangar, fire extinguished. One blind hit, personnel loss.[7]

This is a necessarily brief but accurate account of the battle; however truth and accuracy were not what was required in the fevered atmosphere of a Nazi high command which had much higher expectations.

At 19.30 on the 1st Kummetz was summoned to the telex connection to Narvik for a conversation with Admiral Kluber. The conversation opened with a quote from Narvik of a message for Kummetz which had been received from C-in-C *Gruppe Nord*, Admiral Karls in Kiel, and read:

> To BdK and *Lützow* Commander.
> Request an immediate detailed coherent report on *Regenbogen*. This is required urgently for report to a superior department. BdK to comment in detail on the battle group *Lützow*, especially concerning reaction, battle distance, success. Approve formation withdrawal once enemy cruiser resistance identified.[8]

There were at this point communications glitches at various stages along the German chain of command, resulting in Kummetz receiving increasingly strident requests for detailed information from several sources, including some passed via the cruiser *Köln* anchored nearby. After clarifying what Admiral Kluber had or had not received by way of reply, Kummetz went on to state his position again, particularly concerning reports not sent by himself as the commander at sea, and his use (or lack of use) of the battle group destroyers:

1. Initially I would like to establish that I cannot understand how the impression of a great success could arise at home. If there is no success I will not report it. It did not occur to me to specifically report that there is *no* success. If an impression arose as a result of a submarine commander's report stating that he saw crimson, this is not my responsibility. I could no longer correct this impression as I was in retreat [and maintaining radio silence].
2. I think one does not appreciate the difficulties connected with the task given. I had no doubts about them at any time. Experience gained during exercises and at war have shown that it takes a considerable length of time to fight down guarding armed forces, even if they are only destroyers and they act skilfully. Only on rare

103

occasions does one succeed in getting to the steamers within a convoy before the guarding armed forces have been fought down.

3. The time which was available to me was very limited. There are virtually only two hours of rifle light [twilight] in this latitude per day . . . My last advance onto the convoy at approximately 11.00 hours with the *Hipper* and *Lützow* groups, in loose tactical connection with increasing darkness, already involved a risk that I could only take heavy-heartedly in view of the instructions given to me . . .

4. Therefore undivided attention had to be given to torpedo risk during these light conditions. I considered it to be wrong to approach closer because of torpedo risk. I slowed *Hipper* commander down on one occasion and approve of *Lützow*'s conduct during his battles.

5. It was necessary to keep the groups together, meaning the destroyers with the cruisers, as otherwise any control would have been lost. I only once managed to set the *Eckholdt* group on an immobilised destroyer [*Bramble*]. This task was taken on by *Eckholdt* single-handedly. He took quite some time with it. As he was about to connect he met an enemy cruiser group . . . It appears that he believed he had connected with *Hipper* whilst it was in fact English cruisers . . . This instantly highlights the difficulties which existed in recognising friends, enemies and types. What is more this was a very reliable, experienced and exceptionally efficient flotilla commander. It would therefore have been wrong to release the destroyers, as control would have been lost and it would have been virtually impossible to get back together . . .[9]

Kummetz had evidently heard of the message of 11.45 on the 31st despatched by *Kapitänleutnant* Herschelb of *U354*, and the interpretation of great success which had been put upon it by a German high command which, accordingly, had anticipated his confirmation of the destruction of the convoy with heady anticipation. While his explanation puts his point of view clearly, it is also apparent that he is becoming rattled and irritated by the impression that a witch-hunt is in progress higher up the chain of command concerning the unexpected lack of any positive results. He is also naturally concerned that if scapegoats are required, neither *Kapitän zur See* Stange (whom he loyally supports) nor himself, should be blamed for carrying out their instructions not to risk the heavy ships.

In a later report Kummetz stated candidly his opinion concerning the lack of results – 'The operation's objective could possibly have been achieved if the imposed commitments had been ignored. On the other hand this would always have involved high risks for the cruisers. A radio message, which I received whilst already at sea, placed particular emphasis on avoiding high risks.'[10]

Vice-Admiral Kummetz's explanations were considered, logical and reasonable, but it is difficult to escape the conclusion drawn by *Kapitän zur See* Stange that this engagement had been a missed opportunity: 'When our vessels leave the battle area it is with the uneasy feeling that, despite the overall situation, which seemed so favourable to begin with, we have not succeeded in getting close to the convoy, neither did we achieve any success at all.'[11]

New Year's Eve at Wolfschanze (Wolf's Lair), Hitler's headquarters in the forest close to Rastenburg, East Prussia, was turning out to be an unexpectedly jovial occasion. As 1942 drew to a close it appeared that military operations had taken a significant turn for the worse, particularly on the eastern front where General von Paulus' Sixth Army stood in danger of being surrounded at Stalingrad. Nevertheless, as the *Führer* greeted his guests he bubbled with excitement at the news that an Arctic convoy had been destroyed – a message had been received from a U-boat observing the battle, and he expected details imminently. Instructions were given to issue a grand announcement to the media on New Year's Day.

As the evening wore on Hitler became increasingly edgy and constantly quizzed Admiral Krancke for news. Krancke in turn contacted Berlin, who contacted *Gruppe Nord,* who contacted Kluber in Narvik, who could get no reply from Vice-Admiral Kummetz as he steadfastly maintained radio silence until the battle group was safely out of harm's way. Explanations were forwarded that bad weather had delayed the battle group's arrival, the telex link from Norway to Berlin had broken, etc., but by the morning of 1 January Hitler's mood had turned to fury. With impeccable timing, it was at this point that his information bureau brought him a transcript of a BBC news broadcast which claimed that units of the Royal Navy, escorting a convoy in the Barents Sea, had put to flight a superior German force on New Year's Eve – the convoy having escaped unscathed. Hitler boiled over, condemning the German navy for not fighting the action through to a finish (despite his own strictures against taking risks), and declaring that the defeat spelt the end for the German High Seas Fleet. Capital ships, he raged, were a waste of men and *matériel* and served no purpose other than to tie up other much needed forces for their defence. In a towering fury he ordered Berlin to contact the battle group immediately and get news of what had happened. Despite this, by 17.00 on the 1st there was still

105

no word (the telephone and telex links still not having been re-established), and Hitler again sent for Admiral Krancke. Raging at the unfortunate admiral that the failure to produce a report was an affront to his person as the *Führer* of the *Reich*, Hitler declared: 'I have made the following decision, and order you forthwith to inform the Admiralty that it is my unalterable resolve. The heavy ships are a need-less drain on men and materials. They will accordingly be paid off and reduced to scrap. Their guns will be mounted on land for coastal defence.'[12]

In the face of this onslaught Admiral Krancke courageously attempted to dissuade the *Führer*, but Hitler was not to be placated and issued instructions for Grand Admiral Raeder to report to him immediately in person. Staff at the Admiralty in Berlin warned Raeder that trouble was brewing, and made an excuse that he was unwell and would be unable to travel to Wolfschanze for a day or two. Thus granted a few days' respite Raeder was able to prepare himself for the conference, but the time was also used by his old sparring partner, *Reichsmarschall* Goering, to poison the atmosphere further by complaining to Hitler that *Luftwaffe* squadrons were being 'wasted' guarding the big ships, and reinforcing the notion that they should be scrapped. It is sometimes difficult to believe that Goering and Raeder were on the same side. It is even more difficult to believe that Hitler put up with Goering's bluster for as long as he did.

The meeting between Grand Admiral Raeder and Hitler finally took place at Wolfschanze on the evening of 6 January 1943. Also present were Field Marshal Keitel, Chief of Staff Armed Forces High Command, and two stenographers. Without giving Raeder a chance to put his case, Hitler launched into a 1½-hour tirade against the German navy from its inception to the existing hostilities. Again ignoring the fact that it was his own reluctance to risk the capital ships which prevented them from being used more often, he complained that in the present situation 'where all fighting power, all personnel, and all *matériel* must be brought into action, we cannot permit our large ships to ride idly at anchor for months'.[13] Forging on he repeated Goering's belief that *Luftwaffe* squadrons were wasted protecting the big ships, and continued by displaying his total lack of understanding of naval warfare, declaring that 'until now light naval forces have been doing most of the fighting. Whenever the larger ships put to sea, light forces have to accompany them. It is not the large ships which protect the small, but rather the reverse is true.'[14] Finally coming to the point Hitler reiterated his belief that the heavy ships should be paid off and scrapped, and instructed Raeder to prepare a memorandum covering the following points:

1. Should the three aircraft carriers which were planned, be retained? Should other ships be converted into aircraft carriers? Are *Hipper* and *Prinz Eugen*, because of their great speed, more suited than *Lützow* or *Scheer*, which have a more extensive operating radius? If the latter were lengthened, could they develop greater speed and could they be given a larger landing deck?
2. Where would the heavy guns of these ships best be mounted on land?
3. In which order should the ships be decommissioned? Probably *Gneisenau* would be first, since she will not be ready for active duty until the end of 1944. Next would probably be the ships which are now due for overhauling and repairs. Personnel of these ships will remain with the navy.
9. Can the submarine programme be extended and speeded up if the large ships are eliminated?[15]

Enduring the tirade in more or less silence, the aristocratic Raeder believed that this had been an attempt to humiliate him personally, and accordingly 'considered it beneath my dignity to refute his statements'.[16] The Grand Admiral now requested a private talk with Hitler, and Keitel and the stenographers left. Raeder was a sound strategist who, in the years leading up to 1939, had warned Hitler of the particular problems to be faced on entering military conflict with a naval power such as Britain. Following the outbreak of war he further warned Hitler against the military adventure into Russia, at least until Britain had been defeated. Now, however, he felt that it was time for the *Führer* and himself to part company, and offered his resignation as C-in-C of the *Kriegsmarine*. He was, after all, he said, almost sixty-seven years old and there were younger admirals, now with the necessary war experience, to take his place.

Hitler immediately began to back-pedal, insisting that he had not intended to criticise the navy as a whole, only the big ships. Furthermore Germany was sustaining heavy losses in Russia, and the *Führer* believed there was much criticism of him for dismissing too many generals. It would be highly embarrassing should Raeder now resign as well. Nevertheless, Raeder was adamant, but in order that no criticism should fall on Hitler personally, the admiral suggested that he be given an honorary title, indicating that he was still involved with the navy and that his decision to resign as C-in-C had been amicably agreed. Hitler reluctantly acceded to the request, and the date for Admiral Raeder's stand down was set at 30 January 1943, the tenth anniversary of Hitler's rise to power.[17] Hitler also requested the names of two officers who, in Raeder's opinion, would be suitable successors. Raeder's first choice was Admiral Rolf Karls, his second the C-in-C of the U-boat arm, Admiral Karl Doenitz. Hitler had always stressed the importance of the U-boat campaign, and so appointed Doenitz.

By 15 January Raeder, in conjunction with the naval general staff, had completed and handed in the lengthy memorandum required by Hitler, including what amounted to an 'idiot's guide' to the necessity of retaining battleships and cruisers. The principle of the 'Fleet in Being' demanded that Britain keep substantial units of her fleet at Scapa Flow to cover *Tirpitz* and the other German capital ships, even if they did no more than swing at anchor in the Norwegian fjords. Raeder forcefully maintained that if, as a result of the Battle of the Barents Sea, the battleships and cruisers were scrapped, it would be the cheapest victory that the Royal Navy had ever won. Britain would interpret the scrapping of the ships as a sign of weakness, and of Germany's complete ignorance of the immense importance of naval warfare. Britain, he maintained, whose entire warfare depended upon her dominance of the sea-lanes, would consider the war won if Germany destroyed its ships.[18] However his efforts were to no avail, and Hitler refused to change his mind.

His resignation becoming final, Raeder was given the title Admiral Inspector of the Navy but, as suggested by Raeder himself, this did not involve any further active role.

To welcome the *Kriegsmarine*'s new Commander-in-Chief to his post, on around 30 January Hitler presented Admiral Doenitz with a memorandum outlining his intentions for the German fleet:

1. All construction and conversion of heavy ships is to cease with immediate effect.
2. Battleships, pocket battleships, heavy cruisers, and light cruisers to be paid off, except where they are required for training purposes.
3. The resultant dockyard capacity, workmen, seamen, and weapons (mainly anti-aircraft), rendered available to be applied to an intensification of U-boat repair and U-boat construction.[19]

Admiral Doenitz's initial response was acceptance of this memorandum, particularly with regard to item 3, his specialist area.

As he was quickly to discover however, the crisis for the German navy went much deeper than the proposed scrapping of all its big ships. At this time serious consideration was being given to the idea that much, if not all, of the navy should be transferred to army command. Having just been appointed C-in-C of the navy Doenitz was naturally opposed to the notion, and at the *Führer* conference on sea power held at Wolfschanze on 8 February made a special plea for the U-boat branch, together with all ancillary surface vessels, to remain the province of the navy. Hitler promised to consider the proposal seriously, but indicated that he would need to have further discussions with Field Marshal Keitel before making a final decision.[20] At the same conference, Doenitz submitted his proposals for decommissioning the capital ships. The programme in essence maintained that *Tirpitz, Lützow,* and *Nurnberg* should remain operational in Norwegian waters until August 1943, plus *Scharnhorst* and *Prinz Eugen* in the Baltic, following which they would be progressively decommissioned. *Prinz Eugen, Scheer, Leipzig* and *Emden* would have minimal repair and maintenance works carried out, to enable them to be used as training ships. Dates for decommissioning definitely proposed were:

Cruisers *Admiral Hipper* and *Köln* 1 March 1943
Battleship *Schleswig-Holstein* 1 April 1943
Battleship *Schlesen* 1 May 1943
Battlecruiser *Scharnhorst* 1 July 1943
Battleship *Tirpitz* autumn 1943.[21]

This would release 250 officers, 92 of whom could transfer to the U-boat service, and 8000 petty officers and men, who would be dispersed to the U-boat service, coastal and flak batteries, and replacements for the remaining surface ships. It was estimated that 1300 dockyard workers would also become available for work on the smaller surface ships (destroyers etc.), and for U-boat repairs. Hitler approved the plan.

Having assisted with the drawing up of plans for what amounted to the destruction of the German navy, Admiral Doenitz began to have second thoughts. A submarine specialist through and through, he had a somewhat myopic view of sea power, but he was nobody's fool, and on becoming Commander-in-Chief began to see the bigger picture and appreciate the value of the 'Fleet in Being'. He was also (unlike Raeder) a political animal perfectly prepared to play power politics at the Nazi court. At this he proved to be extremely adept, successfully fending of the army's attempts to take control of the navy. He also determined to try to save some of the capital ships, and at the next conference on sea power, at Vinnitsa on 26 February 1942, broached the matter with Hitler, skilfully opening the discussion by using one of the *Führer*'s complaints to support his case. The *Führer*, Doenitz maintained, had correctly decided that Germany could not afford to have her big ships lying idle. As a result *Hipper*, *Leipzig* and *Köln* had been decommissioned, to be followed shortly by further ships. Doenitz went on to explain that he considered the Allies' Russia convoys to be excellent targets for the big ships, and considered it his duty, in view of the desperate fighting on the eastern front (comparing the eastern front to the efforts of the navy was another Hitler hobby horse), to exploit the possibilities to their fullest extent. The admiral therefore proposed to strengthen the naval forces in Norway by transferring *Scharnhorst* from the Baltic, which, combined with *Tirpitz, Lützow* and the destroyers already there, would make a powerful task force. Hitler was not to be easily persuaded however, and retorted that he was strongly opposed to any further operations by the surface ships. Since the sinking of *Graf Spee* one defeat had followed another. Large ships, he maintained, were a thing of the past, and he would prefer to have the steel and nickel contained in them than sanction their use again.[22]

Doenitz shifted his ground while still attempting to use Hitler's arguments against him, maintaining that the big ships were severely hampered by the restrictions imposed that they must not be damaged or sacrificed. Hitler declared that he had never issued such an order (which was correct – he had, nevertheless, made his feelings clear on the subject many times, which in Nazi Germany amounted to the same thing as an order). Hitler went on to state that if in contact with the enemy, ships must go into action, but in any event he no longer valued their effectiveness. Mounting his hobby horse, he bemoaned the sacrifices made by the men on the eastern front while the strength of the Russians was constantly increased by the convoys, the most recent of which comprising twenty-five ships (*JW53*), had just reached its destination. Doenitz seized on this to press his case, declaring that instead of decommissioning *Tirpitz* and *Scharnhorst*, he considered it his duty to send them into action whenever possible for as long as suitable targets could be found.[23]

Hitler reluctantly agreed to despatch *Scharnhorst* to Norway and asked how long it would be before a suitable target could be found. Doenitz replied that he thought it would be within the next three months, to which Hitler taunted, 'Even if it should require six months, you will then return and be forced to admit that I was right.'[24]

1   PRO. DEFE 3/215, and Kummetz, Vice-Admiral Oskar *The Diary of Operation Regenbogen*, Bundesarchiv.
2   Kummetz, op. cit.
3   Ibid.
4   Brennecke, Jochen *Eismeer, Atlantik, Ostee.*
5   Ibid.
6   Kummetz, op. cit.
7   Ibid.
8   Ibid.
9   Ibid.
10 Ibid. It is possible that the 'radio message' which Vice-Admiral Kummetz mentions here is the three word morse message which German accounts refer to, but is more likely to be the message sent by Admiral Kluber at 11.45 and received by Vice-Admiral Kummetz at 12.55 (see p. 100).
11 Stange, *Kapitän zur See* Lützow *War Diary*, Bundesarchiv.
12 Bekker, Cajus (1974) *Hitler's Naval War*, MacDonald & Jane's.
13 PRO. ADM 116/5623
14 Ibid.
15 Ibid.
16 Raeder, Dr Erich (1957) *My Life*, Tubingen.
17 Ibid.
18 Ibid.
19 Kummetz, op. cit.
20 Stange, op cit.
21 Ibid.
22 Ibid.
23 Ibid.
24 Ibid.

CHAPTER 9

CONCLUSIONS

That the Battle of the Barents Sea had been a significant victory for the Royal Navy was recognised by both sides. For the *Kriegsmarine*, Vice-Admiral Weichert later commented that their lack of success had been 'due to poor visibility and the problems inherent in a night action, but primarily the Germans were paralysed by the stringency of their operational orders'.[1]

Vice-Admiral Kummetz's plan had been a good one and came close to being successful (had Force 'R' arrived any later, the problems for the defending destroyers would have been acute), but the German forces were indeed hamstrung by the crippling restrictions placed upon them, and also by the confusion of purpose, and perhaps consequent confusion of mind, which resulted from springing Operation *Aurora* on *Kapitän zur See* Stange and *Lützow* a matter of hours before engaging *JW51B*.

By contrast, Captain Sherbrooke, and subsequently Commander Kinloch, both had a clear grasp of their objective, which was in all cases the safety of the convoy. The tactics laid down by Captain Sherbrooke were aggressive and played upon the known caution displayed by commanders of German heavy ships when faced with torpedo attacks. The fate of the battleship *Bismarck* in 1941 undoubtedly underlined this caution. When in a position to make her escape to one of the French Atlantic ports, she suffered a hit to her rudder from a torpedo launched by a Swordfish aircraft. Unable to manoeuvre she was caught and sunk by units of the Home Fleet.

An essential element of Sherbrooke's defence, and the one which as much as anything foiled Kummetz's attack, was the refusal of the escort to be drawn away from the convoy. Despite facing a heavy cruiser and her consorts, Captain Sherbrooke split his own small force of four destroyers by despatching two back to the convoy as he could not pinpoint the whereabouts of the German destroyers, and feared that they might attack the merchantmen. At all times, therefore, and regardless of all difficulties, the safety of the convoy was the prime objective. Commander Kinloch displayed this same singleness of purpose on taking command from the wounded Sherbrooke, and as each attack by German forces was driven off, the British destroyers would fall back to cover the convoy. The contrast with the relative inaction of the German destroyers is stark, and mystified Commander Kinloch, who stated in his report: 'The inactivity of the German destroyers is inexplicable. They made no attack on the convoy and in two engagements were following astern of their cruiser without taking any part.'[2]

Vice-Admiral Kummetz's reasons for not giving them a more active role have some validity, but come firmly under the heading 'playing safe'. That *Kapitän zur See* Stange held the same views was possibly even more damaging to the fortunes of the German operation. Napoleon had been a great believer in luck, and it was undoubtedly a significant piece of luck for the Allies that a snow squall should obscure the convoy at around 10.45, just as the *Lützow* squadron moved into position to attack. However, had *Kapitän zur See* Stange taken the opportunity to launch his destroyers at the merchantmen at that time they must have achieved significant success, as only two corvettes and the badly damaged *Onslow* were available to oppose them at the head of the convoy.

Unaware of the crisis that the battle had caused within the German navy, the Commander-in-Chief Home Fleet, Admiral Tovey, nevertheless felt that it was a job well done, stating in a memorandum dated 25 January 1943:

> The conduct of all officers and men of the escort and covering forces throughout this successful action against greatly superior forces was in accordance with the traditions of the service. That an enemy force of at least one pocket battleship, one heavy cruiser and six destroyers, with all the advantage of surprise and concentration, should be held off for four hours by five destroyers and driven from the area by two 6" cruisers, without any loss to the convoy, is most creditable and satisfactory.[3]

Underlining the fact that his handling of the close escort had not been an isolated piece of good luck, Captain Sherbrooke continued his career with the Royal Navy, subsequently achieving the rank of Rear-Admiral.

The large-scale scrapping of the heavy ships of the German fleet threatened by Hitler ultimately never took place. Nevertheless, three modern cruisers and two old battleships were decommissioned, and work planned to repair the modern battle cruiser *Gneisenau* was put on hold indefinitely. On its own terms the Battle of the Barents Sea had been a notable victory for the Royal Navy, ensuring the arrival in Murmansk, without loss, of convoy *JW51B*. Add to this the crisis caused in the *Kriegsmarine*, and it takes on a much greater significance, dramatically underlined by the subsequent performance of the heavy ships. Admiral Doenitz had promised to find a target for *Scharnhorst* within three months, but in fact it was not until Christmas Day 1943, almost a full year after the Barents Sea action, that the battlecruiser sailed to attack convoy *JW55B*. Units of the Home Fleet, including *Sheffield*, *Jamaica*, and the battleship *Duke of York*, subsequently caught and sank her off the North Cape. The big ships of the German navy did not participate in any further offensive naval operations for the remaining years of the war.

Of the two major warships employed by the German navy in the Battle of the Barents Sea, the flagship, *Admiral Hipper*, left Altenfjord in January 1943 to return to Wilhelmshaven ostensibly for repairs. In April 1943 she passed through the Kiel Canal and transferred to Pillau where she remained, decommissioned, until 1944. Her next and final operation took place in the closing months of the war. In conjunction with a number of other ships brought out of mothballs, she assisted with the evacuation of two million German refugees from the path of the rapidly advancing Red Army, transporting soldiers and civilians from East Prussia and the Courland Peninsula across the Baltic to western Germany. On 3 April she was bombed in Kiel, and on 3 May 1945 she was scuttled.

Lützow remained in Norwegian waters until September 1943, subsequently transferring to Gdynia, where she lay more or less idle until early 1945. The pocket battleship finally became part of the 2nd Battle Group, formed to offer naval support for army operations against the Soviet advance along the Baltic coast, and in this capacity engaged in coastal bombardments, also assisting with the transportation of army personnel, *matériel* and refugees across the Baltic. On 16 April 1945 she was hit during an air attack and left two-thirds submerged. As salvage was impractical, she was blown up to prevent her capture by the Russians.

Vice-Admiral Kummetz had been a sea-going officer since the 1930s, and following the Barents Sea action became C-in-C North Norway Naval Squadron, flying his flag in *Tirpitz.* By the end of the war he was Supreme Commander-in-Chief, Supreme Naval Command, Baltic, being extensively involved in the organisation of the evacuation of German troops and civilians from the path of the Russian armies.

Prior to his appointment to the command of *Lützow Kapitän zur See* Stange had been a section leader with the Supreme Naval Command, and afterwards returned there as Chief of Staff, Naval Group Command South.

The convoys continued to Russia, although they were cancelled during the summer of 1943*. The principal reason for this was a lack of escorts, as the Battle of the Atlantic at that time approached its climax, and had to take precedence. The Russians were not overjoyed at the prospect of no convoys for several months, but in truth the crisis had by that time passed on the Russian front. Soviet industry had settled in the eastern provinces (see appendix I), and set about producing simple but sturdy weapons of war in massive quantities. Stalingrad had been the catalyst. Following the surrender of General von Paulus's Sixth Army, the Russians went over to an offensive which would ultimately take them to the heart of Berlin; the war of attrition on the eastern front bleeding the German army of much of its manpower, ultimately making D-Day and final victory possible. The Russia convoys, and the battles fought in defence of them, played an indispensable part in that victory.

1   G.H.S.4. German Surface Ships. Policy and Operations. Quoted in PRO. ADM 234/369
2   M. 052539/43. Quoted in PRO. ADM 234/369
3   PRO. ADM 199/73

* Convoys were also suspended from May to July 1944 as all available escorts were required for D-Day.

OUTLINE DETAILS OF GERMAN WARSHIPS WITH NOTES ON DEVELOPMENT AND WARTIME CAREERS

Heavy Cruiser Admiral Hipper
Vice-Admiral Oskar Kummetz's Flagship for the
Battle of the Barents Sea
Outline Specification[1]

Built:	Blohm & Voss Shipyard, Hamburg
	Laid down 1935
	Completed 29 April, 1939
Dimensions:	639 ft 9 in (195 m) × 69 ft 9 in (21.26 m) × 15 ft 6 in (4.72 m) draught
Displacement:	Nominally 10,000 tons (10,160 tonnes), standard. Actual displacement closer to 14,900 tonnes
Main Armament:	8 × 8 in (203 mm) in four twin turrets
Anti-aircraft Armament:	12 × 4.1 in (104 mm)
	12 × 1.46 in (37 mm)
	Also a number of 2 cm light a/a guns
Torpedo Tubes:	12 × 21 in (533 mm) in four triple units situated on main deck, 2 abaft bridge, 2 abaft mainmast
Aircraft:	4. Hangar placed between funnel and mainmast 1 catapult
Machinery:	3 sets geared turbines (plus diesels for cruising), to 3 propeller shafts. High-pressure La Mont boilers
	Maximum 80,000 SHP, giving 32 knots
Mines:	Mine-laying capability, for which track was kept onboard
Complement:	830

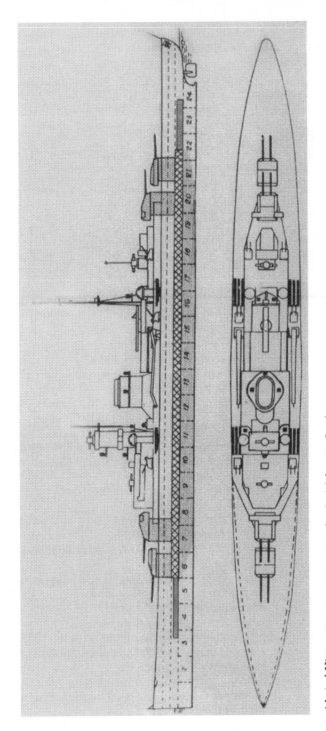

Admiral Hipper (Reproduced with permission from Jane's Information Group)

Pocket Battleship Lützow *(ex* Deutschland*)*
Outline Specification[2]

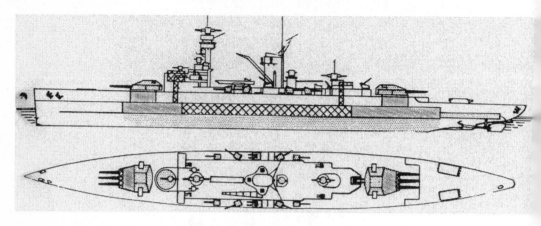

Lützow (Reproduced with permission from Jane's Information Group)

Built:	Deutsche Werke
	Laid down 5 February 1929
	Completed 12 November 1934
Dimensions:	609 ft 3 in (185.7 m) × 67 ft 6 in (20.57 m) ×
	21 ft 8 in (6.63 m) draught
Displacement:	Nominally 10,000 tons (10,160 tonnes), but
	probably over 12,000 tons (12,192 tonnes)
Main Armament:	6 × 11 in (279 mm) in two triple turrets
	New Krupp model firing a 670 lb (304 kg) shell
	Maximum range 30,000 yards (27,432 m)
	Maximum elevation 45°
Secondary Armament:	8 × 5.9 in (146 mm), in single turrets
Anti-aircraft Armament:	6 × 4.1 in (104 mm)
	8 × 37 mm
	10 machine-guns
Torpedo Tubes:	8 × 21 in (533 mm) in two quadruple units aft
Aircraft:	2 (1 catapult)
Machinery:	8 × 2 stroke double-acting diesels (compressor-less), geared to 2 propeller shafts
	Maximum total 54,000 BHP
	Maximum speed 26 knots
	Maximum cruising range at 15 knots 20,000 nautical miles, or 10,000 nautical miles even at high speed
Complement:	926
Note:	Electrically welded hull used for the first time in a ship of this size

Maasz class destroyer Friedrich Eckholdt
(sister vessels Richard Beitzen &Theodor Riedel*)*
Outline Specification[3]

Built:	Blohm & Voss, 1937
	Richard Beitzen Deutsche Werke, 1935
	Theodor Riedel Germania, 1936
Dimensions:	374 ft 0 in (114 m) × 37 ft 0 in (11.28 m) × 9 ft 3 in (2.82 m)
Displacement:	1625 tons (1651 tonnes), standard
Main Armament:	5 × 5 in (127 mm), in five single turrets
Anti-aircraft Armament:	4 × 37 mm
	4 × 20 mm
Torpedo Tubes:	8 × 21 in (533 mm) in two quadruple units
Anti-submarine Armament:	Depth charges
Machinery:	Geared turbines. High-pressure water tube boilers
	Maximum 50,000 SHP, giving 36 knots
Complement:	283

Type 1936A (Mob) Narvik class destroyers
Z29, Z30, Z31 [4]

Built:	1941/42
Dimensions:	410 ft 0 in (125 m) × 39 ft 4 in (12 m) × 9 ft 6 in (2.90 m)
Displacement:	2603 tons (2645 tonnes)
Main Armament:	5 × 5.9 in (146 mm), in one twin and three single turrets. Some (e.g. *Z30*) fitted with a lighter single turret forward to improve seagoing characteristics
Anti-aircraft Armament:	4 × 37 mm
	4 × 20 mm
Torpedo Tubes:	8 × 21 in (533 mm) in two quadruple units
Machinery:	Geared turbines. Designed 55,000 SHP giving 36 knots

Articles 181 and 190 of the Treaty of Versailles severely limited post-First World War development of the German navy, a central provision restricting German 'battleships' to a maximum 10,000 tons displacement, whereas the Washington Naval Agreement of 1922 restricted the size of battleships of the major naval powers (Britain, France, Italy, Japan and the United States) to 35,000 tons. As the time for replacing the older battleships Germany had been allowed to keep in 1918 approached, the problem greatly exercised the planners and architects of the German navy. The solution arrived at proved

119

to be unique and in many ways revolutionary – the aptly nicknamed 'pocket battleship'. The basic premise was actually quite simple – to build a vessel fast enough to outrun more heavily armed enemy battleships, yet with sufficiently powerful main armament to outgun enemy heavy cruisers which had a faster turn of speed.

The first of this new class of vessel, the *Deutschland*, caused quite a stir in naval circles (see outline specification). Her combination of range, speed, and firepower made an ideal commerce raider, and commerce raiding, it was decided, would be the main aim of the German navy in any future conflict with Great Britain. Two sister vessels followed the *Deutschland*, the *Admiral Scheer*, one of the most successful German surface raiders of the Second World War, and probably the most familiar of the three, *Admiral Graf Spee*.

Innovative she may have been, but *Deutschland* was not a lucky ship. On 24th August 1939, just prior to the outbreak of war, and three days after *Graf Spee* sailed on her fateful voyage, *Deutschland* departed Wilhelmshaven for her 'waiting area' off the southern tip of Greenland. On the outbreak of hostilities with Britain she proceeded to her 'hunting ground' in the North Atlantic between the Azores and the North American coast. In early October she sought prey in the busy Caribbean shipping lanes, and on the 5th, some distance east of Bermuda and taking care to remain outside the Panamerican Neutrality Zone, she sank the British SS *Stonegate*, 5044 gross tons. Off Cape Race on 9 October she captured the steam tanker *City of Flint*, which, it transpired, was United States owned. This was something of an embarrassment as the United States was at that time neutral, and the German regime was not yet ready to antagonise another potential enemy. This embarrassment was compounded when the officer sent from *Deutschland* with a prize crew sailed the vessel to two neutral ports, Tromsoe and Murmansk, where she should have been impounded for the duration of the war; however, she was subsequently allowed to return to the United States. On 14 October *Deutschland* sank the Norwegian SS *Lorenz W. Hansen*, 1918 gross tons, east of the northern tip of Newfoundland.

Following the Battle of the River Plate and the sinking of *Graf Spee*, Hitler began to develop that mental twitch which always seemed to affect him when German heavy ships were operational, and therefore at risk. He became extremely concerned at the possible effect on public morale should a warship with the name *Deutschland* be sunk, and she was therefore ordered home, arriving at Gotenhafen on 15 November subsequently to be renamed *Lützow*.

Concerned for the continuation of essential iron ore supplies from northern Sweden via Norway, and aware how useful Norwegian ports would be to the *Kriegsmarine*, Hitler ordered the invasion of Norway and Denmark. On 9 April 1940 the troops went in, and for her first sortie under her new name *Lützow* was ordered north in support. Off the Skaw on 11 April she was hit in the stern by a 21 in torpedo from the British submarine HMS *Spearfish*,[5] the damage proving to be serious, and almost fatal, for she nearly foundered while under tow to Kiel. In dry dock her stern was stripped down and completely rebuilt, the repairs and subsequent trials taking over a year to complete.

Operationally effective again at the beginning of June 1941, *Lützow* was once more ordered north to Norwegian waters (something of a nemesis for this ship). Off Egersund, *en route* to Trondheim, she was hit amidships by an 18 in torpedo from a solitary RAF Beaufort torpedo bomber. Developing a list, she altered course and headed through the Skagerrak, proceeding at 16 knots back to Kiel. Entering dry dock immediately she remained under repair until mid-November 1941, when she left for trials in the eastern Baltic.

May 1942 saw *Lützow* once more in Norwegian waters, this time for anti-convoy operations. Ordered to join her sister ship *Admiral Scheer*, the battleship *Tirpitz* and heavy cruiser *Admiral Hipper*, for an attack on convoy *PQ17*, she grounded in fog while leaving Ofotfjord bound for Altenfjord.[6]

Having repaired in Trondheim she spent some time in the Baltic, but by December 1942 she was back in Norwegian waters for operations against Russia-bound convoys in the Barents Sea.

Dr Erich Raeder became Commander-in-Chief of the German navy on 1 October 1928, and managed to retain his post under the Nazi regime. Raeder was a sound naval strategist who appreciated the complexities of sea power, but he was not prepared to indulge in the manoeuvrings and political machinations necessary to achieve prominence at the Nazi court, concerning himself only with the affairs of the *Kriegsmarine*. As a result he never obtained admittance to Hitler's inner circle of confidants and advisers, a factor which may have had a negative effect on the ability of the *Kriegsmarine* to wage the kind of war which would be necessary, since Hitler's attitude to his navy was at best ambivalent. He was fascinated by the big warships as military hardware, appreciating the prestige they brought to the *Reich* from abroad, but his conviction that capital ships and aircraft carriers were the 'playthings of the decadent democracies'[7] ensured pre-war emphasis on the production of U-boats for the navy and aircraft for the *Luftwaffe*. Both achieved much, but Raeder believed that the addition of aircraft carriers and more surface raiders could have stretched the Royal Navy to breaking point.

Underlying Hitler's dealings with Raeder were his suspicions concerning the officers and men of the *Kriegsmarine* – after all, had not the sailors of the High Seas Fleet mutinied in 1918? In his eyes this constituted a fatal and unforgivable stab in the back for the German nation. By 1938 Hitler appeared to have come around to Raeder's way of thinking, inviting proposals for an expansion of the fleet and assuring Raeder, as he had done previously, that there would be no war with Britain until 1944 at the earliest. The result was the Z Plan, in which Raeder envisaged a balanced fleet of capital ships, aircraft carriers, U-boats and support vessels, achievable by 1944. By 1939 however, Hitler became convinced that there was nothing to be gained by waiting. Any improvement in German arms would be offset by increased military preparations now being put in hand by her enemies.

When war came in 1939 the *Kriegsmarine* consequently found itself caught between two stools. On the one hand there were not enough U-boats in service to cut Britain's supply routes, and on the other the surface fleet was nowhere near ready for fleet actions with the Royal Navy. U-boat production was increased during the war years, and although for Admiral Karl Doenitz, Commander-in-Chief of the U-boat arm there were never enough, for the Allied merchant and naval seamen who had to take them on, there were more than sufficient.

In commerce-raiding terms much was expected of *Lützow* and her sister vessels, but other designs were not so suitable. Excessive fuel consumption, limited cruising range and unreliable engines, for instance, seriously hampered the heavy cruiser *Admiral Hipper*.

The outbreak of war saw *Admiral Hipper* at Kiel, where she remained, with the exception of brief visits to Pillau in October 1939 and Hamburg in December 1939, until 31 January 1940. Having dry-docked at Wilhelmshaven on 10 February she sailed in company with the battlecruisers *Scharnhorst* and *Gneisenau* on her first operational sortie, to intercept Allied shipping leaving the north Scottish islands and the Clyde. The operation was compromised two days out by an encounter with a British submarine, and the force returned to Wilhelmshaven.

Supporting the invasion of Norway in April 1940, *Admiral Hipper* sailed north to land troops and equipment at Trondheim. Also in the area, the ageing British battlecruiser *Renown* and four destroyers were similarly bound for Norway. The destroyer *Glowworm* became detached from the squadron in fog while searching for a man overboard, and on the morning of 8 April sighted *Admiral Hipper* and supporting vessels. While trying to make her escape, *Glowworm* came under accurate fire from the German heavy cruiser and suffered several hits. With his ship on fire, *Glowworm*'s captain, Lieutenant-Commander Roope, determined that he could do better than abandon her without responding to the German force. He therefore turned the burning destroyer toward the German battle group and rammed her into *Hipper*'s bows, tearing a 120 ft (36.6 m) gash in the cruiser's side and letting in 528 tons (536 tonnes) of water. However, in the process *Glowworm* was dragged under *Hipper*'s bows and sank. Roope was awarded a posthumous VC for his action. Although the German cruiser developed a 4° list to starboard she was able to proceed with her mission, and successfully landed men and *matériel* at Trondheim.

Having returned to Germany for repairs, May 1940 saw *Admiral Hipper* back in Norway. On 13 June she was attacked by British naval aircraft and again damaged, returning once more to Germany for repairs. Her next sortie, in September that year, was a commerce-raiding cruise in the North Atlantic, but once again she got no farther than the Norwegian coast when engine trouble forced her to return. In December 1940 she tried again, encountering convoy *WS5A* off the west coast of Africa, *en route* to the Middle East via the Cape of Good Hope. Tracking the convoy from late on Christmas Eve, *Hipper* attacked early on Christmas morning but ran into the cruiser escort, *Berwick, Bonaventure* and *Dunedin.* There was some exchange of fire, one merchant ship was damaged and *Hipper* also received some minor hits. The action was brought to a halt when the German heavy cruiser found herself again plagued by engine trouble and broke away to the north. This sortie was on the face of it a failure, but it had an unforeseen knock-on effect. Included in the *WS5A* convoy were five fast merchant ships under the code name Excess which, instead of going around the Cape, were to leave *WS5A* at Gibraltar and proceed at speed through the Mediterranean with troops, airmen and crated Hurricane fighters for Malta, plus supplies for Greece.

When *Hipper* attacked, orders were given for the convoy to scatter, and the Excess ships were held at Gibraltar. Excess finally sailed on the evening of 6 January, some ten days later than anticipated, escorted by Force 'H' – the battlecruisers *Renown* and *Malaya,* aircraft carrier *Ark Royal,* cruiser *Sheffield* and six destroyers (the size of the escort for five merchant ships illustrates graphically how urgently the supplies were required). On the evening of the 9th Force 'H' turned back for Gibraltar, handing the convoy on to the cruisers *Gloucester* and *Southampton,* strengthened later that day by the main escort under the command of the C-in-C Mediterranean, Admiral Cunningham, in the battleship *Warspite,* with the battleship *Valiant,* aircraft carrier *Illustrious,* and seven destroyers in attendance.[8]

Excess had been delayed for ten days or so as a result of *Admiral Hipper's* abortive attack, and during that time an important change had taken place in enemy dispositions in the Mediterranean. Fretting that the Italians were not pressing the British hard enough, on 10 November Hitler wrote to Mussolini proposing that *Luftwaffe* units should operate from Italian bases against British shipping. *Il Duce* agreed, and by Christmas 1940 the unit chosen, *Fliegerkorps X,* was moving down through Italy. By 8 January ninety-six bombers had arrived at bases in the south from which they could strike at Allied shipping, to be strengthened by the end of January to 120 long-range bombers, 150 dive bombers and 40 fighters. *Fliegerkorps X* were the *Luftwaffe* anti shipping specialists.[9]

The newly arrived *Luftwaffe* units struck the convoy and escort on 10 January, concentrating most of their attack on *Illustrious.* Seven direct hits and three near misses crippled the carrier, turning her into a blazing wreck – but for her armoured flight deck she must surely have been sunk. Suffering a further attack on the way, the severely damaged ship managed to reach Gibraltar where she was patched up and sent to the United States for repair. She would be out of the war for over a year. The merchant ships all reached their destination, but the crippling of *Illustrious* was a serious blow to the balance of naval power in the Mediterranean.[10]

Following her attack on *WS5A, Hipper* arrived at Brest on 27 December, was repaired, and was at sea again on 1 February 1941. Her prey now were convoys from Britain to the United States and the Mediterranean, her operational area between the latitudes of Gibraltar and south-west Ireland. Chronically high fuel consumption meant that the first order of business on arrival was to refuel at sea from a supply ship; however on 11 February her luck changed when she sighted the unescorted, laden, UK-bound convoy *SLS64*, comprising nineteen merchantmen. The cruiser subsequently sank seven ships totalling 32,806 gross tons, and damaged four more.[11]

Back at Brest on 14 February *Hipper* became the target of British bombers but escaped damage. As persistent engine problems necessitated a return to Germany for a major refit, on the night of 15/16 March she slipped away from France and having refuelled at sea off southern Greenland, passed through the Denmark Strait on 23 March, heavy weather shielding her from patrolling British warships waiting for just such an opportunity to catch German raiders heading to or from the Atlantic.[12] Having had to refuel again, *Admiral Hipper* arrived at Kiel on 28 March. Her unreliable engines and short cruising range made her particularly unsuitable for operations in the Atlantic, consequently she was relegated to a long period of training exercises in the Baltic.

By March 1942 *Admiral Hipper* was *en route* to northern Norway, and on 5 July, in company with *Tirpitz* and *Admiral Scheer*, she sailed from Altenfjord to attack convoy *PQ17*, but when the convoy scattered the battle squadron was recalled, and the attack was left to U-boats and the *Luftwaffe*, (see pp. 10–12).

The heavy cruiser remained based in northern Norway, carrying out minelaying operations off the north-west coast of Novaya Zemlya in the eastern Barents Sea in September, and from 5 to 9 November, in company with destroyer *Z27*, sank the Russian tanker *Dombass* and anti-submarine vessel *No.78*. Recurring engine problems prevented several proposed sorties to attack independently routed merchant ships bound for Russia, but she was scheduled to attack the next Russia-bound convoy discovered in the Barents Sea.

During the German invasion of Norway, British naval forces attacked a large German destroyer force in Narvik, and in battles fought over two days, 16–17 April 1940, sank the entire complement of ten ships for the loss of two of their own. As replacements, the *Kriegsmarine* designed and built what were intended to be the most powerful destroyers in the world. Popularly referred to as the Narvik class, after the ships lost in Norway, they weighed in at 2600 tons and boasted five 5.9 in (150 mm) guns, against the 4.7 in (120 mm) to 5 in (127 mm) guns of the more powerful of the British or American destroyers. Unfortunately for the *Kriegsmarine* this significant increase in fire-power led to other drawbacks with the design. The forward two 5.9 in guns were carried in a twin turret weighing a massive 60.4 tons (61.37 tonnes), compared to the 25-ton (25.4-tonne) twin turrets of the British Tribal class destroyers. This meant that the German boats were prone to dip their bows into the sea under the weight, while yawing and proving very difficult to handle in a following sea.[13] To improve seagoing characteristics some were fitted with a lighter single turret forward, replacing the heavy twin mounting. An additional, and it would seem fairly obvious, drawback with the large guns was the weight of the shells, which, at 100 lb (45 kg), had to be loaded by hand – a considerable physical strain for the gun crews. Due to their difficult heavy-weather handling these ships were not best suited to operations in the Arctic; nevertheless five were sent to Norway to support the naval build-up.

The U-boats were undoubtedly the German navy's most successful and most feared ship-killers, however ultimately they also suffered terrible losses. Of the 40,000 men enlisted into the submarine service, 30,000 were killed. *U354*, which shadowed and unsuccessfully attacked convoy *JW51B*, is a case in point. A Type VIIC boat, she was commissioned on 22 April 1942 at the Flensburger Schiffsbau shipyard, carried out twelve patrols, sank three ships for a total of 19,899 gross tons, and damaged two more totalling 6134 gross tons. Two incidents aboard *U354* underline the hazardous nature of sub-marine warfare, quite apart from enemy action. On 11 November 1942 *Fahnrich zur See* Horst Mayen was lost overboard, and on 12 March 1943, in an incident not uncommon in the U-boat service, *Maschinenmaat* Helmut Richter committed suicide.[14]

However, not all was doom and gloom. Late on 31 December 1942 as *U354* reconnoitred the Barents Sea battle area, Admiral Kluber in Narvik took time to send good news to one crew member: 'To: Herschelb. For Lt. E. Rainer. Its arrived. Going well Dora. Best Wishes.'[15]

On 24 August 1944 two British corvettes, a frigate, and a destroyer, tracked *U354* and sank her with all hands in the Barents Sea. *Kapitänleutnant* Herschelb, whose message of 31 December 1942 unwittingly helped to cause the seismic upheaval in the German navy following the Battle of the Barents Sea, had previously transferred and was not with the boat at the time.

On the outbreak of war with Germany, Soviet industry was capable of manu-facturing large quantities of basic but reliable and sturdy weapons of war – guns, tanks, aeroplanes, etc. The problem was the factories, which were almost all situated in western Russia in the immediate path of the invaders. Had these factories been overrun, defeat for the Soviets would have been inevitable, as resupply from Britain and the United States could not hope to keep pace with all the requirements of the Red Army. The solution was both breathtakingly simple and enormously complex. The Russians would move all the plant and machinery, entire factories, eastwards away from the rapidly advancing Germans.

In the four months from July to October 1941, 1½ million trucks and 915,000 railway wagons transported over 1000 factories east, together with the manpower to rebuild them, install plant and machinery, and operate them. Some 100,000 men accompanied the dispersion of Soviet industry eastwards, and the results of this enormous physical and logistical exercise were equally impressive. Aircraft factories moved to Saratov began production before the roofs were on – fourteen days after the last jigs were installed, MiG fighters were rolling off the production line. The tank works transported to Kharkov produced its first twenty-five T-34 tanks ten weeks after engineers rebuilt the factories. Winter in eastern Russia is a desperately hard affair; nevertheless despite atrocious working conditions the winter of 1941/2 saw Soviet arms production reach 4500 tanks, 3000 aircraft, 14,000 guns, and over 50,000 mortars.[16] This equipment would be vital in the coming months, but could not hope to keep pace with the rate of attrition on the Russian front. It was vital that the hundreds of thousands of tons of military hardware and equipment scheduled for transportation from Britain in the Arctic convoys were fought through to Russia.

1   (1998) *Jane's Fighting Ships of World War II*, Tiger Books International edition, and Koop, Gerhard & Klaus-Peter Schmolke (2001) *Heavy Cruisers of the* Admiral Hipper *Class*, Greenhill Books, Lionel Leventhal Ltd.
2   (1998) *Jane's Fighting Ships of World War II*, Tiger Books International edition, and Whitley, M.J. (2000) *German Capital Ships of World War II*, Cassell.
3   (1998) *Jane's Fighting Ships of World War II*, Tiger Books International edition.
4   (1993) *German Naval Vessels of W.W.II*, compiled by US Naval Intelligence, Greenhill Books, Lionel Leventhal Ltd. and Bekker, Cajus (1974) *The German Navy 1939–45*, Reed International Books Ltd.
5   PRO. ADM 223/289
6   PRO. ADM 223/369
7   PRO. ADM 116/5623
8   Winton, John (1998) *Cunningham*, John Murray (Publishers) Ltd.
9   Ibid.
10   Ibid.
11   It should be noted that entries in *Admiral Hipper*'s War Diary maintain that she sank fourteen of the nineteen ships in *SLS64*, total tonnage approaching 80,000 gross. Given that the convoy was unescorted this is perfectly possible, and if correct would make it the most devastating attack on a convoy by a single warship. It is also possible that the British admiralty might only admit the sinking of seven ships, believing that the loss of fourteen to attack from a single warship would have serious morale implications. However, this is speculation.
12   Humble, Richard (1971) *Hitler's High Seas Fleet*, Pan/Ballantine.
13   Bekker, Cajus (1974) *The German Navy 1939–45*, Reed International Books.
14   http://www.uboat.net/boats/u354.htm
15   PRO. DEFE 3/215
16   Pitt, Barrie & Frances (1989) *The Chronological Atlas of W.W.II*, MacMillan.

OUTLINE DETAILS OF BRITISH WARSHIPS WITH NOTES ON DEVELOPMENT AND WARTIME CAREERS

Southampton class light cruiser Sheffield
Rear-Admiral Robert Burnett's Flagship, Force 'R'
Outline Specification[1]

Built:	Vickers Armstrong, Barrow
	Laid down 1934
	Completed 25 August 1937
Dimensions:	584 ft 0 in (178 m) × 61 ft 8 in (18.8 m) × 17 ft 0 in (5.2 m)
Displacement:	9100 tons (9246 tonnes)
Main Armament:	12 × 6 in (152 mm) in 4 triple turrets, at the time of the Barents Sea action. As the war progressed all the Southampton class had 'X' turret removed and replaced by two quadruple Bofors anti–aircraft mountings
Anti-aircraft Armament:	10 × 20 mm fitted 1941, replacing original multiple machine-guns
	16 × 2 pdr pompoms
Torpedo Tubes:	6 × 21 in (533 mm) in two triple units
Aircraft:	2 Walrus seaplanes, one housed either side of the fore funnel, in a hangar abaft the bridge
	1 catapult athwartships
Machinery:	Parsons geared turbines, built by Vickers
	Twin-screw. Admiralty 3-drum boilers
	75,000 SHP, giving 32 knots
Complement:	833

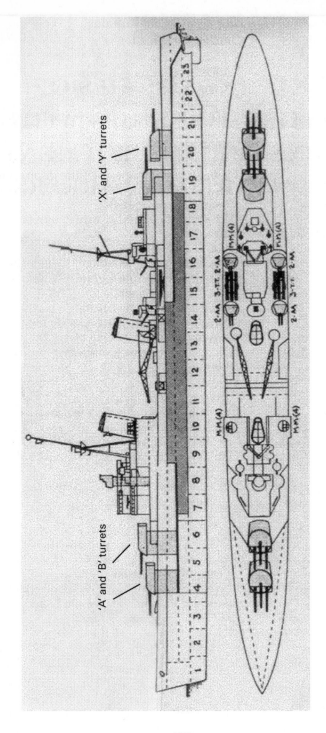

'X' and 'Y' turrets

'A' and 'B' turrets

HMS *Sheffield* (*Reproduced with permission from Jane's Information Group*)

Fiji class light cruiser Jamaica
Outline Specification²

Built:	Vickers Armstrong, Barrow Launched 16 November 1940 Completed 29 June 1942
Dimensions:	555 ft 6 in (169 m) × 62 ft 0 in (18.9 m) × 16 ft 6 in (5 m)
Displacement:	8000 tons (8128 tonnes) War additions such as torpedoes and extra splinter protection caused the displacement to rise to 8631 tons (8769 tonnes), but without compromising speed
Main Armament:	12 × 6 in (152 mm), in 4 triple turrets
Anti-aircraft Armament:	10 × 20 mm
Torpedo Tubes:	6 × 21 in (533 mm)
Aircraft:	2 box hangars abaft bridge, 1 either side of the fore funnel, equipped to carry Walrus and later Sea Otter seaplanes 1 fixed catapult athwartships
Machinery:	Parsons geared turbines. Quadruple-screw 4 Admiralty 3-drum boilers 72,500 SHP giving 31.5 knots
Complement:	980

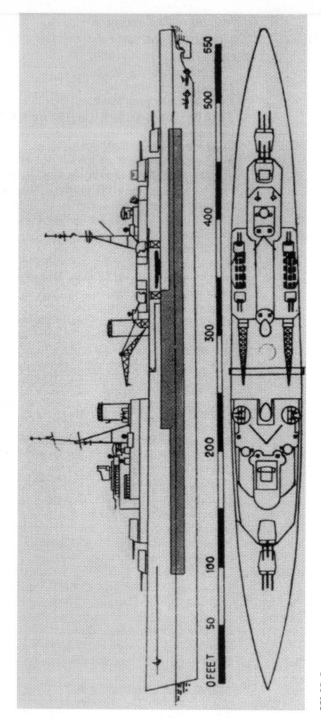

HMS *Jamaica* (*Reproduced with permission from Jane's Information Group*)

'O' class destroyer Onslow
Leader, 17th Destroyer Flotilla,[3] and sister vessels
Obedient, Obdurate, Orwell

Built:	Clydebank, 1941
	Obedient, Obdurate, Orwell, 1942
Dimensions:	345 ft 0 in (105 m) × 35 ft 0 in (10.6 m) × 15 ft 8 in (4.67 m) max
Displacement:	1540 tons (1564 tonnes)
Main Armament:	4 × 4.7 in (119 mm)
	Obedient, Obdurate, Orwell fitted for rapid conversion to minelayers – 'Y' gun and both sets of torpedo tubes could be removed and stored ashore, to be replaced by 60 mines in two racks[4]
Anti-aircraft Armament:	4 × 2 pdr
	8 × 20 mm
Anti-submarine Armament:	4 mortars[5]
Torpedo Tubes:	8 × 21 in (533 mm) in quadruple mounts
Machinery:	Parsons geared turbines to twin-screws
	2 Admiralty 3-drum boilers
	40,000 SHP, giving 34 knots

Acasta class destroyer Achates[6]

Built:	Launched Clydebank 4 October 1929
Dimensions:	323 ft 0 in (98.4 m) × 32 ft 6 in (9.9 m) × 12 ft 0 in (3.65 m)
Displacement:	1330 tons (1351 tonnes)
Main Armament:	Initially 4 × 4.7 in (119 mm) – see anti-submarine equipment below
Anti-aircraft Armament:	Initially 2 × 2 pdr pompoms, 5 machine guns Later replaced by 20 mm a/a guns, and a 12 pdr (see torpedo tubes below)
Anti-submarine Armament:	By 1941 'A' turret replaced by forward throwing Hedgehog a/s mortar, 'Y' turret replaced by additional depth charges
Torpedo Tubes:	Initially 8 × 21 in (533 mm), first destroyers to be fitted with quadruple mounts. Aft bank subsequently replaced by 12 pdr a/a gun
Machinery:	Brown-Curtis HP turbines & Parsons LP twin-screw
	34,000 SHP, giving 35 knots
Complement:	138

Flower class corvettes
Rhododendron & Hyderabad[7]

Built:	Harland & Wolff, Belfast, 1940 & Alexander Hall, Aberdeen, 1942
Dimensions:	205 ft 0 in (62.5 m) × 33 ft 0 in (10 m) × 14 ft 6 in (4.42 m)
Displacement:	925 tons (940 tonnes)
Guns:	1 × 4 in (101 mm)
Anti-aircraft Armament:	1 pompom
	20 mm machine-guns
Anti-submarine Armament:	1 forward-firing Hedgehog multi-barrelled mortar
Machinery:	Triple expansion
	2 SE boilers
	IHP 2750, giving 16 knots
Complement:	85

Halcyon class fleet minesweeper
Bramble[8]

Built:	Launched Devonport Naval Dockyard 12 July 1938
Dimensions:	230 ft 0 in (70.1 m) × 33 ft 6 in (10.2 m) × 7 ft 3 in (2.21 m)
Displacement:	875 tons (889 tonnes)
Armament:	2 × 4 in (101 mm)
	5 machine-guns
Machinery:	2 × 3-cylinder compound steam engines
	Twin-screw
	2 Admiralty 3-drum boilers
	7150 IHP, giving 17 knots
Complement:	80

Trawler Northern Gem[9]
Fitted as rescue ship

Built:	Cochrane, 1936
Dimensions:	173 ft 3 in (52.8 m) × 28 ft 8 in (8.63 m) × 12 ft 6 in (3.81 m)
Gross Register Tonnage:	655
Machinery:	Triple expansion
	1100 IHP, giving 12.5 knots

Britain's economy between the wars depended on her vital trade routes with the empire, and her many other overseas trading partners, the Royal Navy's mainstay for the defence of these trade routes being the cruiser. At the Washington conference of November 1921, pressure was applied to the British delegation, principally by the United States (whose strategic considerations were wholly different from those of Britain), to restrict the number of cruisers in commission. Britain refused but put forward a proposal – which was accepted – that cruisers should not exceed 10,000 tons, and mount guns 8 in (200 mm). The principal concern at this time was not the navy of Germany, but that of Japan, which had undergone major expansion and modernisation and threatened the balance of power in the Pacific.

At the Geneva conference of 1927, a further attempt to limit the potentially damaging naval arms race between the major powers disbanded without agreement, primarily due to Britain's inability to accept restrictions on cruiser strength again proposed by the United States. January 1930 saw a third conference, this time in London, at which Britain finally allowed itself to be persuaded by the United States to accept a reduction in cruiser strength from seventy units to fifty, with a maximum new build programme of no more than 91,000 tons by December 1936. This reluctant agreement was in no small part brought about by the dire economic circumstances in which Britain and most of the industrialised nations of the world found themselves during the 1930s, nevertheless it was to have serious consequences for the outbreak of war in 1939, by which time the Royal Navy would have only sixty-two cruisers to carry out world wide-trade protection and fleet commitments.[10]

The Southampton class cruisers, (later known as Town class), were designed and built to counter the new cruisers of the Japanese navy, and much thought and debate went into the pros and cons of the 6 in (150 mm) gun against the larger 8 in (200 mm) option. The weight of the 6 in shell was, at 100 lb (45.3 kg), less than half that of the 8 in which tipped the scales at 250 lb (113.4 kg). To balance this, twelve 6 in could be mounted against eight 8 in, and a more rapid rate of fire achieved with the smaller gun, giving the 6 in cruiser a superiority in weight of broadside of nearly three to one – 7200 lb (3266 kg) per minute, against the 2500 lb (1481 kg) of its bigger-gunned rival.[11] Despite these advantages the smaller gun could be outranged, requiring the 6 in cruiser to close the enemy as rapidly as possible while having improved armour protection to withstand hits while it manoeuvred into a firing position. Inevitably, higher speed and heavier armour are impossible to equate on a restricted budget, therefore the Southamptons were provided with heavier armour and their speed held at 32 knots.[12] An engagement at night or in poor visibility (dependent upon the efficiency or otherwise of the protagonists' radar equipment) was expected to favour the smaller-gunned ship. The Battle of the Barents Sea falls nicely into this scenario, as *Sheffield* and *Jamaica* were able to close on the larger-gunned *Admiral Hipper* and open fire from comparatively short range.

Sheffield had the distinction of being only the second Royal Navy warship to be equipped with the fledgling radar (or 'radio location' as it was initially known), being fitted with the Type 79 RDF in November 1938. The first vessel so equipped was the battleship *Rodney* in August of that year.

Sheffield had a busy war, and a career which amply illustrates the dual cruiser roles of keeping open Britain's supply routes, plus fleet duties. On 7 April 1940 she accompanied a Home Fleet battle group sent north for the abortive Norwegian campaign, and later that year was transferred to Admiral Sir James Somerville's Force 'H' stationed at Gibraltar. Here she took part in a complicated series of operations designated *Hats, Coat* and *Collar*, which aimed at reinforcing Admiral Cunningham's fleet in the eastern Mediterranean, while passing merchant ships through to supply Malta. As already noted (see appendix I), *Sheffield* accompanied the Excess convoy on the western Mediterranean leg of its trip from Gibraltar to Malta and Greece in early January 1941.

In May 1941 *Bismarck* broke out into the Atlantic, and Force 'H', including the carrier *Ark Royal*, was ordered north from Gibraltar to strengthen the escort of a convoy of five troopships bound for the Middle East. Subsequently brought directly into the hunt, Admiral Somerville detached *Sheffield* to shadow *Bismarck*, and ordered *Ark Royal* to prepare and launch an air strike. Unfortunately the Fleet Air Arm pilots were not notified that *Sheffield* would be in the same area as their target, and attacked the British cruiser. Luckily for *Sheffield* the aircraft used torpedoes fitted with new magnetic detonators, which proved faulty. Of the eleven torpedoes launched, six exploded on impact with the water, and the cruiser managed to dodge the remainder. Ironically this potentially catastrophic case of mistaken identity may have been a blessing in disguise. The torpedo detonators were changed to the old contact type for *Ark Royal*'s next attack, which damaged *Bismarck* enough for a Home Fleet battle group to catch and sink her.

September 1941 saw *Sheffield* and Force 'H' participating in Operation *Halberd*, designed to escort another convoy through to Malta. This was carried out successfully, but the convoy suffered numerous air attacks *en route*, and a torpedo hit damaged the escort flagship, the battleship *Nelson*. The following month the cruiser returned to home waters for a brief spell before being transferred to Arctic convoy duty. On 4 March 1942 she hit a mine and was out of action until July. On completion of repairs convoy duty resumed, with the exception of a brief spell in December when she flew the flag of Rear-Admiral C.H.J. Harcourt, while supporting the *Torch* landings in North Africa.

Following the Battle of the Barents Sea she continued Arctic escort duties until February 1943, transferring to operations in the Bay of Biscay until August, and thereafter supporting the Salerno landings in the Mediterranean. By December *Sheffield* was back in the Arctic, and took part in the sinking of the *Scharnhorst*. In 1944 the cruiser supported raids against *Tirpitz* before being scheduled for a well-earned refit in Boston, Massachusetts. She returned to the UK for completion of the work, and was still under refit when the war ended.

This fine ship remained in service with the Royal Navy until September 1964, finally being disposed of for breaking up in 1967.

In 1937 a second London Naval Treaty restricted cruisers to a maximum displacement of 8000 tons, which, for the Royal Navy meant that construction of the Southampton class could not be continued. A new design conforming to the smaller tonnage restriction was required, and the result was the Fiji class. Various sizes and configurations of main armament were considered, but finally twelve 6 in (150 mm) was adopted, as with the Southamptons.

HMS *Jamaica* spent most of her wartime career on Arctic convoy duty, participating in the Battle of the Barents Sea in December 1942, and the sinking of the *Scharnhorst* in December 1943. Prior to those actions, in company with *Sheffield* she supported the *Torch* landings in North Africa. In 1944 she interspersed convoy escort duties with supporting carrier operations against the Norwegian coast. After the war the cruiser spent time on both the East and West Indies stations, and was part of the 5th Cruiser Squadron in the Far East for the Korean War. Finally paid off, she arrived at Dalmuir on 20 December 1960 for scrapping.[13]

After much discussion the Royal Navy finally accepted the necessity for two distinct types of destroyer, a larger, faster, more heavily armed type for fleet actions, and a smaller type for convoy escort, with the accent on anti-submarine and anti-aircraft armament. It was hoped that this would help to alleviate a chronic shortage in gun production and fire control equipment, which lagged behind the rate at which construction of destroyer hulls was possible.[14] The 'O' class were the first of the new escort destroyers, and to illustrate the dire shortage of guns, with the exception of *Onslow*, were equipped with 4 in (100 mm) main armament, some of which dated back to the First World War.

Since twin gun mountings required power units which would drastically increase top weight, hand-operated single gun turrets were installed, together with hand-operated torpedo tubes, although a powered hoist was fitted for ammunition. Despite these savings the class was still some 80 tons (81 tonnes) overweight (*Onslow* 124 tons – 126 tonnes).[15]

Spending much of their wartime careers on Arctic convoy duty, the class remained in service with the Royal Navy until the mid-1960s.

1   (1998) *Jane's Fighting Ships of W.W.II.*, Tiger Books International, and Lenton, H.T. (1998) *British & Empire Warships of the Second World War*, Greenhill Books.
2   Ibid.
3   Ibid.
4   Lenton, H.T. (1998) *British & Empire Warships of the Second World War*, Greenhill Books.
5   Ibid.
6   (1930) *Jane's Fighting Ships*.
7   *Jane's Fighting Ships* and Lenton, op. cit.
8   (1940) *Jane's Fighting Ships*.
9   (1939) *Jane's Fighting Ships*.
10 Watts, Anthony J. (1999) *The Royal Navy: An Illustrated History*, Brockhampton Press.
11 *http://www.world-war.co.uk/Southampton/southampon* class.htm
12 Ibid.
13 Whitely, M.J. (1999) *Cruisers of World War Two, An International Encyclopedia*, Brockhampton Press.
14 Lenton, op. cit.
15 Ibid.

OUTLINE DETAILS OF THE MERCHANT SHIPS OF *JW51B* WITH NOTES ON THE MERCHANT MARINE

In 1938 (the last period for which pre-war figures are available), 192,372 seamen were employed in the British Merchant Marine, of which some 50,700 were foreign, mainly Indian and Chinese.[1] On the outbreak of the Second World War, Britain's 'Red Duster' flew from 3000 deep-sea cargo ships and tankers plus 1000 coastal vessels, amounting to an impressive 21,000,000 gross tons (21,336,000 tonnes), the largest fleet in the world, comprising 33 per cent of total tonnage. On any one day during the war there would be an average of 2500 British vessels at sea to protect, the rapid rate at which they were lost and had to be replaced becoming apparent when the total sunk, 4700 ships (54 per cent of total world merchant ship losses), is compared to the pre-war total of ships in service.

During the war period some 185,000 seamen served on board British merchant ships, of which 40,000 were foreign, mainly Indian and Chinese although seamen were recruited from other countries, notably the West Indies and Aden. Figures vary, dependent upon which source is consulted, but a reasonably accurate figure for British and foreign merchant seamen who lost their lives as a direct result of enemy action would be 33,000, although it is estimated (but not provable), that the casualty rate might be as high as 25 per cent were it to include those who were wounded, shipwrecked, or otherwise affected, and 'lived permanently damaged lives, still in the shadow of death.'[2]

In the event of sinking, the chances of being picked up were, in the early years of the war, estimated at 3 to 2 against, although the odds improved as time went on thanks to a number of inventions and improvements in the area of life-saving equipment. Of these, three of the most important were:

- the lifejacket light, first supplied in September/October 1940, compulsory from 6 March 1941
- the manual lifeboat pump, first supplied in July 1941, compulsory from 22 July 1942
- protective clothing, first supplied September 1941, compulsory from 27 July 1942[3]

Convoy *JW51B* – Merchant Vessels

NAME	TYPE	TONNAGE	BUILT	OWNERS (MANAGERS)
Ballot (Panamanian Flag)	GENERAL CARGO (Wrecked entrance to Kola Inlet)	6131 gross	1922 ex *Alberta* 1942	United States Maritime Commission
Calobre (Panamanian Flag) (Hit by splinters while under fire from *Lützow* but continued to Murmansk. Vice-Commodore transferred to *Daldorch*).	"	6891 gross	1919 ex *Egremont* 1941	North Atlantic Transport Corporation
Chester Valley (US Flag)	"	5078 gross	1919	Lykes Brothers SS Co. Inc.
Daldorch (British Flag)	"	5571 gross	1930	British & Burmese St. Nav. Co. Ltd (P. Henderson & Co.)
Dover Hill (British Flag) (Returned to UK with weather damage & boiler failure)	"	5815 gross	1918	Dover Hill SS Co. Ltd (Counties Ship Management Co. Ltd)
Empire Archer (British Flag) (Commodore, Captain R.A. Melhuish, RIN)	"	7031 gross	1942	Ministry of War Transport (Raeburn & Verel Ltd)
Empire Emerald (British Flag)	TANKER	8032 gross	1941	Ministry of War Transport (C.T. Bowring & Co.)
Executive (US Flag)	GENERAL CARGO	4978 gross	1920 ex *Carenco*	American Export Lines Inc.
Jefferson Myers (US Flag)	"	7582 gross	1920 ex *Hannawa*	Pacific-Atlantic SS Co. (States SS Co.)
John H.B. Latrobe (US Flag)	" (Liberty Ship)	7191 gross	1942	United States War Shipping Admin.
Pontfield (British Flag)	TANKER (Grounded Kola Inlet but continued to Murmansk)	8319 gross	1940	Field Tank SS Co. Ltd (Hunting & Son)
Puerto Rican (US Flag)	GENERAL CARGO	6076 gross	1919 ex *Golden Tide* 1937, ex *Montague*	American-Hawaiian SS Co.
Ralph Waldo Emerson (US Flag)	"	7176 gross	1942	United States Maritime Commission
Vermont (US Flag)	"	5670 gross	1919 ex *Pacific Hemlock* 1937, ex *West Helix*	California Eastern Line Inc. (Pacific-Atlantic SS Co.)
Yorkmar (US Flag)	"	5612 gross	1919 ex *William Perkins*, ex *West Islay*	Calmar SS Corp.

Delays would often occur between equipment becoming available and becoming compulsory, as time would be required for supplies to be manufactured in sufficient quantities.

During the early stages of the war, the average working week for a seaman aboard a British ship, before overtime, would be ten hours longer than the all-industry average, with shipboard conditions inferior to those of some comparable nations, notably Norway. Nevertheless the Government promptly instituted a war pensions scheme comparable to that of the Royal Navy, while the Ministry of War Transport, the trade unions and owners came together to improve conditions, notably in the area of mail (very important for crewmen), health, general comfort and conditions of life both in the UK and abroad.

Wages also improved dramatically, although while a single man with nothing to spend his money on during long periods at sea might have seen some benefit from these increases, a married man with a family in Britain to support would have to contend with a dramatic 83 per cent increase in the cost of living between 1939 and 1943. Nevertheless, in the first three and a half years of war a British able seaman's pay almost trebled:

3 September 1939 – £9. 12s 6d per month.
1 January 1941 – £17. 12s 6d per month.
1 February 1943 – £24. 0s 6d per month.[4]

These amounts include a 'war risk' (danger money) payment of £3 rising to £10. In addition to these incremental improvements, paid leave and continuity of employment were introduced for the first time. Foreign seamen were paid less than their British counterparts, a source of understandable friction.

Despite the terrible risks involved, there was never a serious shortage of crewmen during the war years, but the same cannot be said of ships for them to sail. By November 1939, the whole of the Belgian fleet had been made available to Britain plus half the Norwegian and Dutch fleets; however, as the German invasion of Europe spread an average of 26 per cent of the Norwegian, Dutch, and Belgian fleets were caught in their home ports and captured. Following the fall of France in June 1940, approximately ½ million tons of French shipping came into British hands, unfortunately matched almost exactly by tonnage of British ships caught in French ports at the same time. Danish shipowners proved to be generally pro-German, and ordered their ships at sea to put into neutral ports, but despite this a number of Danish ships found their way to the UK and operated under British flag, crewed by Danes, for the duration of the war. Greek ships later became an important addition to the fleet.

Formal possession of the ships of the British fleet remained unchanged for the war years, although the Government, through the agency of the Ministry of Shipping (incorporated into the Ministry of War Shipping in May 1941), had, by the summer of 1940, requisitioned all vessels and agreed terms with their owners.[5] This for the most part left crewing, maintenance, and the day-to day running of the ships to the owners, while all decisions as to cargoes and destinations were taken by the Ministry.

By the spring of 1941 a serious shortage of tonnage had manifested itself as a result of war losses. As a consequence, Britain's annual imports dropped sharply from 42,000,000 tons (42,672,000 tonnes) to 28,500,000 tons (28,956,000 tonnes) – less than had been imported in the dark days of 1917. Britain's *minimum* requirement for her civilian population alone amounted to 25,000,000 tons (25,400,000 tonnes) p.a. in addition to which it was estimated that 7–8 tons (7.1–8.1 tonnes) of supplies would be required to support every soldier in Europe when the time for an offensive came – double for the Pacific. To help alleviate the problem, the United States released quantities of old laid up tonnage to Britain on bareboat charter – in which the charterer, in this case the British government, in return for paying a correspondingly low charter rate to the owner, agrees to accept the lion's share of the risks, and crews and operates the ship as the owner in all but name. The United States further assisted by requisitioning all French, Italian, and Yugoslav ships held in US ports and turning them over to Britain. In 1943 another tonnage crisis was eased when the United States agreed to divert ships from the Pacific to the Atlantic.[6]

That the Allies were able to keep the convoys going at all is due in no small part to the Second World War phenomenon the Liberty ship. This British-designed, 10,800 ton deadweight,* 11 knot, 3-cylinder steam-engined cargo ship was enthusiastically adopted by the United States Maritime Commission (USMC) which, however, altered the propulsion system from coal- to oil-fired, and to drastically cut building time, changed the hull design from all riveted to all-welded construction. The USMC also instituted a system of prefabrication whereby sections of ships would be constructed at sites all over the country and transported to the shipyards for final assembly. Placing orders in private and government-owned shipyards in the United States, the USMC built 5777 of these amazingly versatile ships between 1939 and 1945, with design configurations varying from the basic general cargo freighter to tankers, hospital ships, floating repair shops and tank transports ('zipper ships').

This phenomenal effort represents the most prodigious shipbuilding programme ever undertaken, accounting for a total of 56,300,000 deadweight tons (57,200,800 tonnes), at a cost of $13 billion, and constitutes one of the most significant contributions made by any nation to the eventual winning of the Second World War.[7]

The basic premise behind the Liberty ships was to build them faster than it would be possible for the Axis powers to sink them. It was said that they were 'built by the mile, and chopped off by the yard', and indeed one Liberty ship is recorded as having been launched 4 days and 15½ hours after her keel

---

* The deadweight of a merchant ship equates to the tonnage of cargo carried plus banker fuel and luboils, when fully loaded.

was laid. This rapid rate of build inevitably caused a few problems, particularly as inexperienced workers often manned shipyards during the war years. Liberties experienced a high percentage of defects, and 1 in 30 suffered major hull fractures.[8]

Britain placed orders for Liberty ships in US yards, and built similar-sized ships of various standard design types in British shipyards. Adoption of the faster welding method was slow in coming however, and most British-built ships were riveted, although a nod towards modern methods was made with the utilisation of a prefabrication system similar to that in the United States. A significant proportion of ships built in the UK were coal-fired, for the understandable reason that Britain had a considerable coal resource to draw upon. Canada took the opportunity to expand its shipbuilding capacity, and had considerable success in producing standard cargo ships, with designs which tended to follow the British types, but a construction method which favoured welding over riveting.[9] While it would have been impossible to meet the vast tonnage requirements without the massive industrial capacity of the United States, it is also true to say that the US alone could not have met the demands, and the substantial building and repair programmes put in hand by British and Canadian shipyards were vital contributions to ultimate victory.

It was calculated that if a Liberty ship made one loaded trip across the Atlantic she had done all that could be expected, and was unlikely to survive another. The rate at which they would be sunk by the enemy, or would in all probability fall apart due to the way in which they were constructed, would see to that. Despite these pessimistic predictions, war-surplus Liberty ships were snapped up by commercial shipping companies at knock-down prices after the war, and many a fortune was made with them. Liberty ships were to be seen plying the trade routes of the world until the early 1970s, and such was the success of the type that as they came at last to the end of their colourful careers, shipyards around the world fell over themselves to produce designs for 'Liberty replacement types'. The best-known UK version proved to be the Austin & Pickersgill SD14, which kept the same basic design but with a diesel engine, a deadweight increased to just over 14,000 tons (14,224 tonnes) and much improved cargo handling gear.

Of the convoys to Russia, Admiral of the Fleet Sir Dudley Pound commented that they were 'a most unsound operation, with the dice loaded against us in every direction'[10]. Despite this a total of 4,430,000 tons (4,500,880 tonnes) of essential equipment and foodstuffs were transported by this method, although ship losses were higher than on any other Allied convoy route – 7.8 per cent eastbound, 3.8 per cent westbound (in ballast).

A quarter of all Allied supplies to Russia were carried in the Arctic convoys, but the United States sent almost half its total aid to Russia across the Pacific to Vladivostock, carried in Russian ships which, as Russia was not at war with Japan, travelled largely unmolested.

1   (1995) *The Oxford Companion to the Second World War*, Oxford University Press.
2   Behrens, C.B.A. (1955) *History of the Second World War, Merchant Shipping & the Demands of War*, HMSO.
3   Ibid.
4   Ibid.
5   *Oxford Companion*, op. cit.
6   Ibid.
7   Ibid.
8   Sawyer, L & W. Mitchell (1970) *The Liberty Ships*, Newton Abbot, quoted in *The Oxford Companion*, op cit.
9   World Ship Society.
10 *Oxford Companion*, op. cit.

SELECT BIBLIOGRAPHY

Behrens, C.B.A. (1955) *History of the Second World War: Merchant Shipping and the Demands of War*, HMSO.

Bekker, Cajus (1974) *The German Navy 1939–45*, Reed International Books Ltd.

Bekker, Cajus (1974) *Hitler's Naval War* MacDonald & Jane's.

Brennecke, Jochen *Eismeer, Atlantik, Ostsee*, German Publication.

Humble, Richard (1974) *Hitler's High Seas Fleet*, Pan/Ballantine Books.

Kemp, Paul (1993) *Convoy! Drama in Arctic Waters*, Arms & Armour Press.

Koop, Gerhard and Peter Schmolke (2001) *Heavy Cruisers of the Admiral Hipper Class*, Greenhill Books, Lionel Leventhal Ltd.

Pelling, Henry (1999) *Winston Churchill*, Wordworth Editions.

Pitt, Barrie and Frances (1989) *The Chronological Atlas of World War II*, MacMillan.

Pope, Dudley *73 North*, Weidenfeld & Nicholson.

Ruegg, Bob and Arnold Hague (1993) *Convoys to Russia 1941–1945*, World Ship Society, revised edition.

Slader, John (1995) *The Fourth Service, Merchantmen at War 1939–45*, New Era Writer's Guild (UK) Ltd.

Smith, Michael (2000) *Station X*, Channel 4 Books.

Toland, John (1997) *Hitler*, Wordsworth Editions.

van der Vat, Dan (1988) *The Atlantic Campaign, The Great Struggle at Sea 1939–1945*, Hodder and Stoughton.

Watts, Anthony J. (1999) *The Royal Navy: An Illustrated History*, Arms & Armour Press, Brockhampton Press.

MAPS

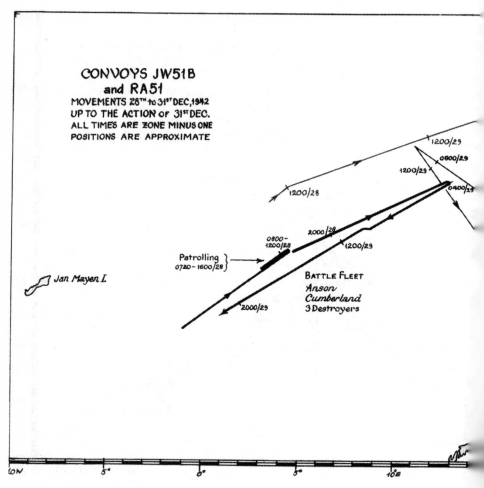

Map A – Movements 28–31 December *(PRO. ADM. 234/369)*

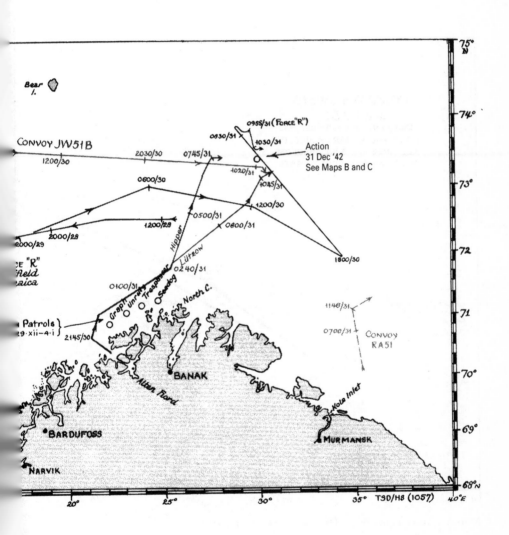

Bear I.

Convoy JW51B

1200/30   2030/30   0745/31   0955/31 (Force "R")
                                  0830/31   1030/31
                                            1020/31   Action
0600/30   1045/31   31 Dec '42
                                                       See Maps B and C
2000/28   1200/28   0500/31   1200/30
2000/29   0800/31
ce "R"   1500/30
field
aica   0240/31
                Lützow
0100/31   Hipper
        Grasp Unruly Trespasser Seadog   North C.   1146/31
Patrols }   0700/31   Convoy
29·xii-4·i   RA51
2145/30

                        BANAK
            Altan Fiord
                                          Kola Inlet
Bardufoss   Murmansk

Narvik

20°   25°   30°   35°   T3D/H8 (1057)   40°E

75° N
74°
73°
72°
71°
70°
69°
68° N

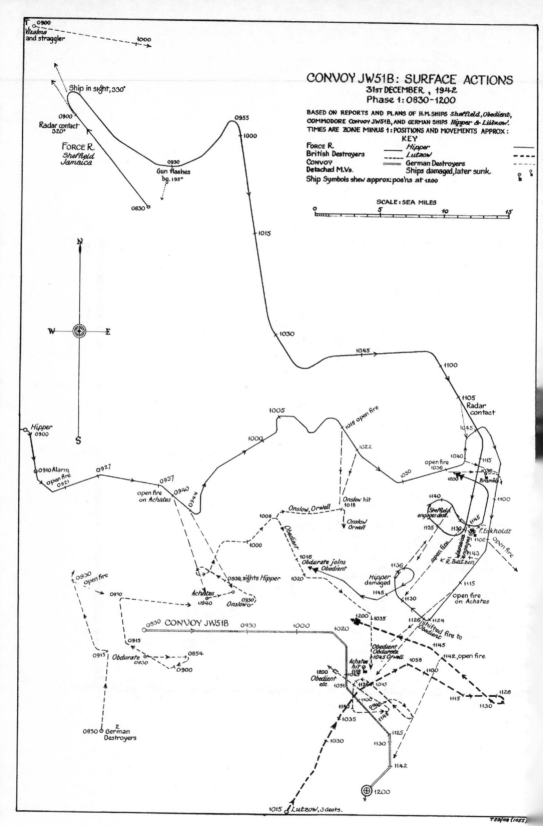

Map B – Surface actions 08.30–12.00 hrs, 31 December *(PRO. ADM. 234/369)*

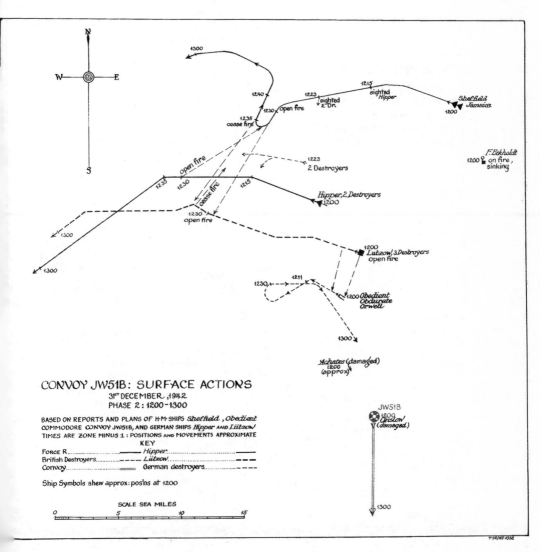

Map C – Surface actions 12.00–13.00 hrs, 31 December *(PRO. ADM. 234/369)*

147

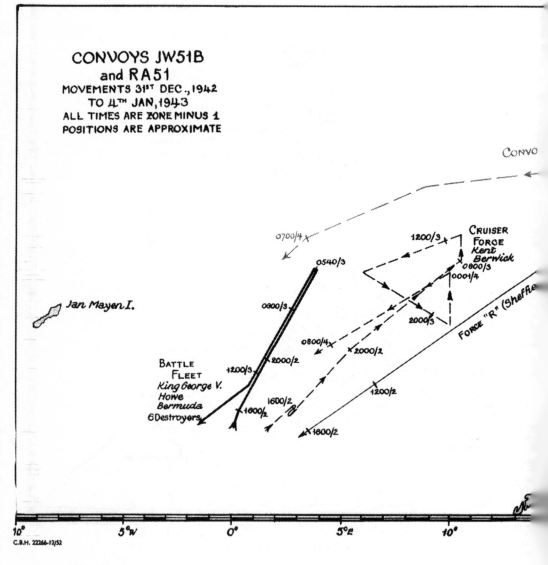

Map D – Movements 31 December – 4 January *(PRO. ADM. 234/369)*

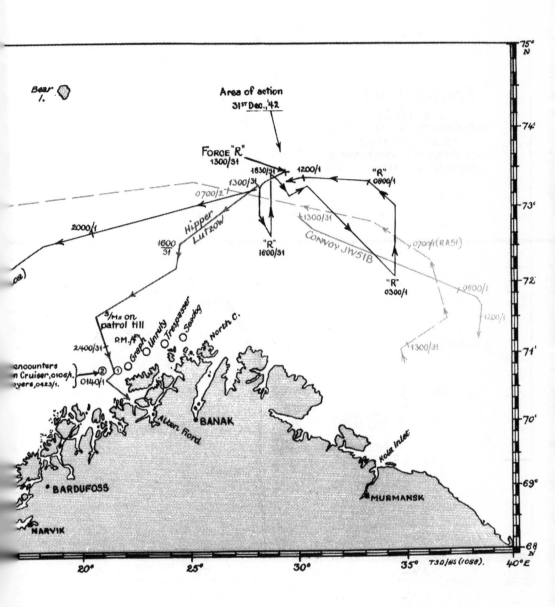

149

INDEX

Page numbers in *italics* refer to illustrations